# Conversations With The Lord: The Blessings of an Intimate Relationship With God

Lydia B. Talley

Unless otherwise noted, Scripture quotations are taken from the Holy Bible, New
International Version, NIV. Copyright 1973, 1978, 1984 by Biblica, Inc. Used by
permission of Zondervan. All rights reserved worldwide. www.zondervan.com
Other Scripture quotations are from the following sources:
The King James Version (KJV). The New King James Version (NKJV). 1982 by
Thomas Nelson, Inc. Used by permission. New American Standard Bible (NASB),
The Lockman Foundation 1960, 1962, 1963,1968, 1971,1972,1973, 1975,
1977,1995. Used by permission. All rights reserved.

ISBN: 0692971513
ISBN 13: 9780692971512
Library of Congress Control Number: 2017919789
Lydia Talley, Prairieville, LA

# Table of Contents

# Introduction

My present journey with the Lord started in 1998, after I began to see Him move in the life of my closest friend, who had rededicated her life to Jesus the year before. I had watched Suzette with skepticism and then amazement as profound changes occurred in her and her family. I listened as she kept sharing the good things that God was doing in her life. I wanted to have what she had: a close, loving relationship with Him within which I could be loved and accepted without having to pretend that I was someone I knew I wasn't. I had never had that type of relationship with anyone and wanted it desperately. So, at forty-seven years old, I asked Him to come into my heart and be my Lord and Savior.

That was the beginning of my relationship with God, our Father; Jesus Christ, our Lord; and the Holy Spirit, our Comforter. For you to have a better understanding of the radical transformation that took place in me that moment, I want to share with you how spiritually lost I was until that time in my life.

When I was in my twenties, my mom and younger sister both experienced salvation and became born-again Christians. I was not impressed or moved by this seemingly bizarre happening in their lives. I was absolutely certain they had made a huge mistake, and I wanted no part of it. I was ignorant and completely unaware that God's plan for my salvation included the faithfulness of those two Godly women to stand in the gap for me—which they did for twenty-five years! I will eternally be grateful to my mom, Pat, and my sister Bev for never giving up on me or our siblings. During those twenty-five years, I had been married, had three children, divorced, earned a college degree, moved away, married again, earned a second degree, and had another child. All of this happened without me purposefully involving God in my decision-making process. Subsequently, without Him, I was not the kind of wife or mother that my family deserved, and I was absolutely not the person that God had ordained me to be. I do know now that He used all of my decisions (wise and foolish) to supernaturally move me in the direction He knew would bring me to Him.

Once I accepted Jesus as Lord, attending church to worship and hear His Word became like water to me. I soaked up everything offered. I was in love with the Lord, I read the Bible, and I prayed off and on throughout the day. But even after my salvation, I struggled to commit a consistent period in my day to seeking Him. What was missing was the level of commitment it took to put Jesus Christ first before all else in my life. My life already seemed to be filled to overflowing with my husband, family, and career. I had a young child, I was a counselor in the public school system, and I had a private counseling practice. Admittedly, I was also a very selfish person who, with few exceptions, closely guarded her time.

Off and on over the next twelve years, I periodically made an effort to be more purposeful in my prayer life: setting aside time each morning to spend with the Lord, reading the Word, and journaling to record my thoughts and feelings. But eventually, sometimes very quickly, I would become distracted, or my priorities would change, and my time with Him became less important. About eight years ago, I began to consistently spend time in prayer and reading God's Word. I also began to regularly journal my thoughts, feelings, concerns, and requests to Him. I found that writing down what was on my heart and mind helped to get it out of my head and allow me to see the issues more clearly, which, in turn enabled me to gain a healthier perspective on my life at that moment. Eventually, I began to discern God's voice as He would speak to me concerning the issues and circumstances I was bringing to Him. Like most people probably would, I questioned whether the Lord would actually speak to my heart in such a way that I could "hear" Him. He was so faithful in responding that over time, my monologue became a dialogue, and I found myself engaged in an ongoing conversation with God that still takes place today. I believe that our Father desires to have an intimate relationship with each one of His children, and that can only be accomplished if we are willing to talk to Him and listen for Him. His Word says, "Seek and you shall find." How else will we know that we have found Him unless we hear from Him?

*Conversations with the Lord* is a devotional taken from my journals of the last six years. It was never my desire to publish any kind of book, but it is in obedience to the prompting of the Holy Spirit that I decided to share His life-giving words. These words are His responses to whatever was occurring in my life or in the lives of my family, friends, or clients in that moment. The book is separated into topics because it is meant to be a resource and a reference for the many questions and concerns we have and the situations we find ourselves in as life happens to each of us.

In my counseling practice and in my walk with the Lord, I have a passion to help people realize their worth and value and to help them see themselves as God sees them—and ultimately, to accept themselves the way He accepts them.

I want to glorify the Lord and be a conduit through which He reaches others and brings hope, healing, and salvation to those who will receive Him. My prayer is that those who read this book will come to know the Lord as He truly is: pure love, infinite in His wisdom, and steadfastly faithful. He is our everlasting promise, Jesus Christ.

—Lydia Talley

# Alignment

# Align with God's Desires

resent yourself to Me as an empty vessel so I can fill you with what you need for the journey. Fast and pray to be emptied of yourself. Devote yourself to the study of the Word. As you look for Me, you will find yourself. This is not a regimen or a law. This is My desire for you so that My purposes can be fulfilled through you. Align yourself with My desires. Seek Me in My temple early and often. Then, all you do and all that is asked of you will seem as nothing. You will move through your days with peace and grace.

Joel 2:12, Hebrews 4:12, and Proverbs 4:10–13

# Alignment Produces Fruit

Time is relative to what needs to be accomplished. Your goals must be aligned with My will so that your efforts produce the fruit that I have portioned out for you. All that you do must have a rhythm and a flow that honors and glorifies Me. I want all of who you are to be focused on all of who I am. That includes your mind, body, will, and emotions. When all you are is in alignment with Me, then your time will not be wasted.

Romans 12:2 and Psalm 119:112

# Come into Agreement

orego all your pleasures for Me. Harken to Me and only Me, because your protection is complete. Satisfy your needs at My feet and make known your requests, for I listen intently to you. Bless you, My child, for you are after My heart. Come into agreement with Me in all matters. Seek My wisdom in all things, for I have a way for you to go. Territories will be conquered by this process. Areas that have been blocked will be opened, and all blessings from Heaven shall flow down upon those who follow this path. Make it known to all who ask that I am coming soon. You will see the hand of God in the land of the living. Do not be afraid of that, but rejoice in the truth of it!

Psalm 5:11, Psalm 25:10, Joshua 1:3, and Revelation 22:12

# Press On

I summon My people to Me, for where I go, you will go. I will never leave you or forsake you. Forget what is behind and press on to what is before you. Place your hand in Mine. See how Mine covers yours completely? All that you are and every aspect of your life is important to Me. I do not reject any part of it. Work with Me as I mold you. For I know what it is that I do. The shape we are achieving is a perfect fit for the plan I have prepared for you. Rejoice in Me, for I am God Almighty! Put all your effort to following Me. Marshal your defenses, for the enemy seeks entry. Pay close attention.

Philippians 3:13–14, Matthew 10:30, and Titus 3:4–7

# Depend on Me in All Matters

Align yourself with Me by coming into agreement. Be on guard, for the enemy watches for openings. Fear, jealousy, pride, laziness, and indecisiveness all give him opportunity to move. Depend on Me in all matters. There are no insignificant or inconsequential decisions, for all decisions are steps in a certain direction. What may seem unimportant in the moment will lead you to a crossroads where your decision has a greater impact. Make decisions that will draw you closer to Me. Call on Me in your doubt or confusion. Clarity comes as you seek My face. My wisdom comes as you prepare the way. My peace is gained in this way.

James 4:7, Ephesians 4:27, Psalm 25:4–5, and Psalm 62:5–6

# Failure Not an Option

Call on Me, child. Your voice is music to My ears. You are My love. You would be wise to put aside all thoughts of failure. It is of no avail. You will accomplish all that I have set out for you to accomplish. Line up your thoughts with Mine. They are worthy to be praised. Press on toward the goal I have set for you. I have ensured your journey. Have faith in Me. The road is rocky, but you are surefooted. Your ground is flat because I go before you. Take heart!

Psalm 135:6, Isaiah 14:24, Philippians 3:14, and Isaiah 45:2

# Examine Your Heart

Are you ready to learn the rest of the story? Follow your heart. See where it leads you. The grace I give you is sufficient for the journey. Do not be afraid of what you encounter, for the outcome is already determined. Examine your heart daily with Me. I have full knowledge of its condition and its desires. We will look at your motives together. We will examine what your heart wants and why. Emotional responses produce no fruit, but godly answers do. When we are aligned, your responses come from Me. When we are not, they emanate from your emotions. Your emotions are connected to your thoughts, not Mine. When you experience emotion, look to Me for words. In that way, you are assured that no wound is created.

Luke 12:34, Lamentations 3:40, and Proverbs 12:18

# Spirit of Excellence

Prepare for Me a clean vessel, one that is unadorned and open to receive what I have for you. Do not take time to wash the outside, for that is unimportant. Spend your time examining the inside and allowing Me to cleanse the areas that need My attention. Gentleness and a soft touch is all that is necessary when your vessel is in alignment with Me. A stronger hand is needed when you neglect to maintain the right relationship with Me. See Me as I am. Know Me according to My Word and My Spirit. Perfect your walk. Obedience is the key. Imperfect people can accomplish things in alignment with My will with a spirit of excellence, as My servant Daniel did. What I have placed inside of you allows you to walk perfectly with Me.

2 Timothy 2:21, Matthew 23:25–26, and Daniel 6:3

Call on God

# Your Ever-Present Help

Forecasts of storms and predictions of disasters abound, but My Word stands against all. I am the calm in your storms. I am your strong tower in disaster. Do not doubt My ability to surround and protect My own. I am your ever-present help in time of need. Call out to Me, for I will answer. I know your need before you speak it. I wait for you to turn to Me so I can unleash My power in your life. When you call out, I answer! Nothing separates Me from you.

Proverbs 18:10, Isaiah 25:4–5, and Romans 8:39

# Come to the End of Yourself

**M**y ways are not your ways. People must come to the end of themselves before their need for Me can be recognized. Therefore, I allow events and circumstances to occur that are beyond man's ability to control or fix. This produces or uncovers a need for which man will be compelled to search out an answer. I am the answer! Measure all that the world holds dear as lost, for the blessings of Heaven are more valuable than gold, more precious than rubies. Earthly pleasures are fleeting and momentary. Heavenly rewards are permanent and lasting.

Psalm 38:10, 15 Psalm 119:72, and 1 John 2:17

# Do Not Run from Me

Whosoever waits on Me will be rewarded. Faint not, My child; I am your forever God. I am the one who made you and the one who saved you. Do not make a bargain with the devil because he will always undermine you. I have been here, but you go about your day not recognizing Me. You do not turn to Me, yet I am waiting for you. My words seem to fall on deaf ears, but I have given you ears to hear. Why do you close them to Me? My words will give life and refresh your soul, yet you avoid them. Your sins were known to Me before I formed you in your mother's womb. My plan for you included these times. I do not run from you, and I ask that you do not run from Me. Your courage wavers and your strength wanes. Come to Me! Your heart darkens, so let My light shine on you! Your eyes are veiled, yet My words will tear back the veil with truth. This place where we are was not unknown to Me. I have your answers, and you will not receive them from any other source. I am the fountain of life. My water flows and is never ending.

Romans 16:18–19, 2 Corinthians 7:1, Jeremiah 6:10, and
Psalm 36:8–9

# Surrender Your Pleasures

Blessings upon you, My child. Entertain no thought of failure. That is impossible when I am involved. Truly I say unto you, surrender your pleasures for My plan. You will reap the benefits of abstaining from those things that bring you momentary pleasure but have no lasting value. Come to Me when you are tempted. I have your answer. Do not avoid Me but seek Me out, for I will strengthen you. I will inhabit the moment with you, and it will pass. When you immediately seek Me, none that the enemy sends on assignment will succeed. Guard your heart and mind with My strength and wisdom. He uses your weaknesses to attack, and when you are not focused on Me, he gains entrance.

Titus 2:11–13, I Corinthians 10:13, I Chronicles 16:11, and Ephesians 6:11

# I Am Listening

I am known to the world by name alone. I am better known to My children by My character. I give careful consideration to those who are in need, for I will provide help when asked. Call on Me, and I will answer. You are My child. I love you and wish to bless you. Rest easy in Me, sweet one. There is much more to learn about yourself and others. Stay open to My voice; hear My words and take them in. Pray always in My Spirit. Place your hand in Mine and give Me your heart fully and completely. My robes are large, and there is plenty of room to cover all of My children. I never grow tired or weary of you. Your voices reach to Heaven. I am listening.

Galatians 5:22–23, Ephesians 6:18, and Isaiah 65:24

# I Am Near

Call on Me for your answers, for I am near and listening. Come away with Me. Surrender all, and let me have My way in you. My truth is your truth, dear one. When you know My voice, you are not confused. Do not let the enemy play tricks on you. I will always alert you to his schemes. Be cautious and watchful but do not allow fear to enter into your thinking. It will derail your progress.

Psalm 91:15, Psalm 86:11, and 2 Corinthians 2:11

# The Doorkeeper

Seek Me in the face of all opposition. Hold on to Me. I am the doorkeeper, and I will open or shut all doors. Do not think I am not listening or that I do not see! Fear brings people to their knees in weakness and in worship. Call on Me in times of trouble. Come to Me in your darkness. Sacrifice to Me your time, energy, and your love. Let Me replace yours with Mine. I have a never-ending supply. It is enough to meet all your needs and to fill your heart's desire. When you generously give yourself to Me, I generously give Myself to you. I want all of who you are, My child. I want your mind, body, will, and your emotions. Submit them to me so I can bless you in ways you've never imagined. My gifts are both internal and external. They go hand in hand, one complementing the other. If you desire things and do not desire Me, your things will only bring fleeting pleasure. When you desire Me, I fill all of your needs, which will leave you satisfied and content. You choose. Home is where the heart is. Your heart is at home with Me. I am your shelter, your protection, and your provision.

Revelation 3:7, Matthew 6:33, and Matthew 6:19–20

# Heed My Words

Call on Me, for I am here. There is nothing that I cannot or will not do in you. My plans are good and perfect. Lean on Me in times of trouble. Be on guard, for the enemy watches for an opening. Listen for My instructions and be sensitive to My Spirit. I will lead you down right paths away from the enemy's traps. Acknowledge Me in all your ways. All that you do is under My scrutiny. I examine all efforts for purpose and motive. Do not be afraid of that but rejoice in it. My refining fire is fresh and new and produces a new person. Welcome Me and My instruction. Heed My words and respond accordingly.

Jeremiah 29:11, Isaiah 58:11, and Psalm 66:10–12

# Come!

all on Me. Let me hear your voice raised in praise and worship. Bow down before Me in reverence. Speak to Me of your love for Me and your desire for My presence. Then I will pour out My blessings upon you. Hold on to Me, My child, as we move through this time. It is inevitable for change to take place. I will not change, but that is not true for anything or anyone else. Rely on Me to fill you with what you need to persevere. You can do nothing without the One who saves.

Psalm 100:1–5, Psalm 102:25–27, and Colossians 1:11–12

# Satan's Weapons

Weep not, My child, for I give ample opportunity for all to know Me. Satan has many weapons with which to wage war against Me through My people: fear, anxiety, hatred, hostility, un-forgiveness, and many more. Many are bound to him and kept from Me because they don't know Me. Their lack of knowledge prevents the movement of My Spirit in them. I gave My life for yours! The way out has been in place since I died and rose again. Rejoice that I have made it easy to be saved—all of Me for all of you! I realize you cannot comprehend My ways, but I do not expect you to. Do not spend too much time contemplating that which is a mystery to you. Continue to work toward the goal I have put in front of you, and call on Me for all you need.

John 1:12, Ephesians 6:12, John 3:16, and Luke 24:6–7

# The Protection of the Blood

*L*ay down all that occupies your heart and mind. Set it before Me and ask for what you need and want. My desire is to bless you with answers. My blessings be upon you, My child. You are My own. Come into agreement with Me every day, and let My will be done in you. Be watchful, for the enemy is not unaware of your love for Me. He seeks to destroy you. Keep your guard up and cover yourself with My armor. Peace will prevail, but we must fight the battle first. Come to Me in all things, never relying on your own knowledge or wisdom. Plead My blood over all you cherish. Protect them with the one thing the devil cannot penetrate. Be mindful of his tactics and learn his ways. Do not ignore the signs of his movement.

John 15:7, 1 Kings 3:5, Ephesians 6:13–17, and Revelation 12:11

# Let Me Heal You

Make your peace with Me. Pour out your heart until it is empty of hurts and questions. Do not hold back, for I want to hear your pleas. Let Me visit with you in the dark places of your life. I will lay My hands on your wounds and bring healing to them. My words will sound sweet to your ears, and you will know My goodness and experience My mercy.

Psalm 62:8 and Psalm 103:2—4

# I Will Meet Your Need

Fashioned and formed for My purposes, you are My creation. Therefore, you are beautiful in My sight. Rest on Me. Lean into Me. My shoulders are broad, and My heart is full for you. Come to Me with all you are carrying. Release your cares to Me, and allow Me to guide you. Don't try to find your own way. Seek Me in My temple. Search for Me in your circumstances. You are My child, in whom I am well pleased. These issues that you contend with keep you tied to Me. You seek Me out of your need, and I meet your need. Isn't that My promise to you? Don't grow weary. This is your path.

2 Timothy 1:9, Isaiah 30:21, and Psalm 34:10

# Lay It All Down

Measure out what you are carrying and lay it down before Me. I will pick it up, and it will be no more. When you have emptied yourself of all that is in you, look around and tell Me what is left. I am all that is left. I am all you need. My love, truth, wisdom, discernment, grace, mercy, and light are sufficient to fulfill all your needs, desires, and wants according to My perfect will. I am enough.

Matthew 11:28 and Psalm 68:19

# Comfort in the Storms

My child, let Me be your comfort in the coming storms. They are inevitable but manageable. Do not hide from Me. You are naked before Me at all times, so there is no hiding. Rejoice that I know you so well. There is freedom in that truth, for as I see you, so you are. You make mistakes, but I make the corrections. There is nothing that you do that I cannot undo—and if I choose not to undo it, find hope in My knowledge of it. For there is purpose in all that I do. It is not for you to know all My purposes. Instead, believe in Me and trust in My divine nature. As you grab hold of the truth, you grab hold of Me, and with Me you have all you need, all you desire.

Psalm 107:28–31, Hebrews 4:13,
Philippians 2:13, and Job 42:2

# Release All

eave your cares behind. They are a weight that is unnecessary to carry. Give it all to Me. That has been My eternal offer. Trust in My goodness, My power, and My love. All that I am is all that you need. I am more than powerful enough to heal you and make you whole. I hear you, sweet one. I listen intently. Release all to Me, and then you will know the direction to take, the answer to give, and the peace that is yours through Me. Bind yourself to Me, and pledge your troth to the one, true, and living God. Commit you ways to Me. Secure your peace by honoring Me with your life. Hold fast to My truths, for they will surely set you free.

Psalm 37:5; Psalm 16:2, 5; and Proverbs 16:3

# Commitment

# Fear of Commitment

You need to make major revisions in the manner in which you approach life and live it. Because your focus stays on yourself, your weaknesses, faults, perceptions, and beliefs are highlighted constantly. You never lose sight of you; therefore, you can never truly see Me. You are blocked by yourself. Your need to take care of you supersedes your ability to let go and let Me take care of you. Look closely at the ways you have been avoiding, ignoring, or forgetting My words. There is a stronghold here. The stronghold is your refusal to let go of control of your time. You believe that you will feel forced to do things you don't want to do. You always want the choice to opt out and be able to escape. You have a fear of commitment. When I am truly your center, then you will experience the freedom from bondage that you are searching for.

Proverbs 5:1–2, Isaiah 26:3, and Psalm 91:14–15

# Focus on Others

Wholehearted, no-turning-back, all-in commitment requires more of you than you have been willing to give. It requires unselfish, others-focused abandonment. Your lamp is full of oil. Use it to pour out blessings on others. When you become focused on others, your eyes will clear, and your heart will be free. Don't allow your fear to limit you. My words to you are truth. Eat them and allow them to become a part of you. They will enrich and enhance your life. Test Me in this.

Proverbs 11:25 and 2 Corinthians 9:8–11

# How Deep Is Your Pool?

C all on Me, My child. Never forget who has your answers. My heart is full for you. We measure the depth with a stick fashioned of love and truth; the stick is designed to measure your commitment to Me. How deep is your pool? Be on guard, for the devil watches you. He is not aware of the depth of your pool either, so he believes it is shallow and produces openings. Do not give him any. I have renewed your spirit for a time such as this. My energy feeds you, for you would grow weary without Me. Remember My words—they will sustain you in the future. Come to Me in all things, and never let it be said that you did not seek Me, for I am always ready to respond to you. You are My own, and My own are never left alone and unattended.

Matthew 7:7–8, 1 Thessalonians 3:5, Isaiah 40:30–31, and
Hebrews 4:16

# Let Me Fill Your Time

The next step requires more commitment from you, and you are contemplating what it will mean. You say, "More of You, less of me," but do you really mean it? Make a decision that puts you solidly on one side or the other. Is this all you want of Me? There is so much more available. There is enough to fill your cup to overflowing. Yet you hang back, not trusting Me. Yes, My child, you do not fully trust Me. Your time needs to be Mine also. You jealously guard your time, but where does it come from? Who gave it to you? Do you believe you can use your time better than I can? Do not become complacent. Time is short, but you have all the time in the world to do what I have for you. Use time wisely; understand that procrastination is an attempt to avoid failure. Stop thinking and believing that time is solely yours; it has been and will be a gift from Me. I love you, so let Me fill your time. Honor Me by giving Me control of your time, letting go of the illusion that you are in control. Let Me be God of your time as well as your heart. I want all of you. I am a jealous God.

John 3:30, I Corinthians 2:9, Ephesians 5:15–17, Exodus 34:14

# Divine Presence

# A Constant Companion

You will never be without Me, My child. I am your constant companion. No space or time exists between us. Nothing blocks your way to Me. Seek me in all of your moments, for I have given them to you so you could share them with Me. We share the same space and time; therefore, you can never be alone. Feeling alone is a heart issue and occurs when there is a question of My love for you. When you question My love, you are questioning My character. Trust is the issue, and faith is the answer. Let Me show you who I really am, and I will expose the lies of the enemy that have kept you from knowing Me and prevented you from feeling My presence and receiving My love.

Deuteronomy 4:7, Romans 5:8, and 2 Timothy 2:26

# Rest in My Arms

Passion and promises are part of My plan for you. Because I am passionate about you, I lift you up and enfold you in My loving embrace. I am your Father in Heaven who loves you beyond all measure. As you cannot measure the rain that falls from the heavens, you cannot measure the width and breadth of My love for you. Rest in My arms as you contemplate your life's journey. Trace your steps: the misdirected ones, the faulty ones, the hesitant and tentative ones, as well as the sure and confident ones. I have been with you as you've placed each one. If you were not aware of Me, it is because your eyes were focused elsewhere. Your experiences and circumstances gradually brought your focus back to Me. My presence became clearer and sharper until your mind's eye could see Me in the foreground and not as part of the background—no longer hidden among the millions of other images, thoughts, and experiences.

Ephesians 3:17–19, Joshua 1:5, and Jeremiah 23:23–24

# You Are Never Alone

You are used to measuring out time and distance. Your natural world requires them for order and structure. But measures of time and distance are not necessary in Heaven, for eternity has no need of them. Place your trust in the One who lives eternally, for there is no distance to travel to reach Me, nor is there a certain amount of time needed to ensure contact. I am ever present in the hearts and minds of My people. I give careful consideration to My children, and I give them measures of faith as well.

2 Peter 3:8 and Leviticus 26:12

# The Enemy Has a Plan

Peace be unto you, My child. My peace comes with My presence, but you cannot always feel it because of the many barriers and stumbling blocks the enemy uses to separate My people from Me. Make sure you stay alert and aware of the methods he attempts to use on you. You will notice which areas of your life he attacks and the patterns that take shape from those attacks. Some of the methods he uses to get your attention and interrupt the flow of the life-giving relationship between us are busyness, pride, offense, temptation, rejection, condemnation, emotional pain, unforgiveness, and deception. Make note of these areas so that he doesn't gain ground again. I have won the war, and you reap the spoils of the victory: peace, wisdom, strength, grace, love, and truth. My gifts remain constant. The flow is only interrupted when you don't receive them. That is a heart matter. When you desire to know Me, you will receive. Open your heart to Me so My Spirit can flow in you and through you.

Galatians 5:19–21, James 1:17, and Jeremiah 24:7

# Stay Connected

old on to Me through your day. It is essential that we stay connected. I have given measures of time to you. Use them well. Position yourself to receive My love and instruction. Humble yourself in My presence by inclining your ear to My voice, committing your way to Me, and submitting your will to Mine. I will pour new wine into your new wineskin. Your words will be fresh and clean to open ears, for out of your mouth will flow My Living Water to refresh the spirits and revive the hearts of the dying.

John 15:5, James 4:10, and Luke 5:38

# Faith

# Boldness Is Your Weapon

Hold on to Me, My child. Times are changing, and you will require My strength to endure. Fear should not come into this if your faith is strong. You have been given everything you need for this journey. You lack nothing in My presence. Bind up all thought of failure—failure occurs in the mind before it actually occurs in the natural. Be mindful of that truth. Do not entertain thoughts of failure, for that will impede your progress and trap you in fear. Boldness is your weapon, boldness rooted in Me. Take charge and move forward, for now is your season. Measure out your time to include this effort. Peel off the cover and empty the contents of this blessing. Pour it out on those who will receive. Be joyful! We are moving forward.

Psalm 23:4, Psalm 56:3–4, and Proverbs 28:1

# I Know You

Place your hope in Me. Lay down your worries and fears before Me. Measure out your faith and see where it is lacking. Be assured that I have knowledge of you. You are not unknown to Me, and nothing about you has escaped My notice. Therefore, what I ask of you is not impossible. It may be difficult by your standards, but I do not recognize your standards. My power, anointing, strength, and wisdom are inherent in My commands. You receive all you need when you obey. I am always speaking to you, child. Anything I say can be and needs to be applied to your life. Ingest My words. Do not let them stay as knowledge only. Eat them as fruit; be fed and nourished by them. They are meant to fill you.

Psalm 39:7, Hebrews 13:21, and Jeremiah 15:16

# Faith Overcomes Fear

old fast to these truths. Those who seek Me will find Me. I am in the shadows and in the light. The force of My love will propel you forward. Fear is inevitable, but faith overcomes fear. My Word says, "Fear not!" Heed My Word. When fear comes, seek Me. When you seek Me, you are using the faith I have given you. I will honor your effort and answer with My own. Your faith will deepen, and My glory will be revealed.

Deuteronomy 4:29, Isaiah 41:13, and John 11:40

# My Touch is Permanent

My people yearn for My embrace but do not receive it as it is offered. They do not recognize My touch because they expect it to resemble a human touch. But My ways are higher than man's, so My touch will never feel human. It will be supernatural and speak to their "knowing" rather than their feelings. Feelings are temporary, but when I touch one of My own, it is permanent. It becomes part of their faith experience, and they are changed by the knowledge of it. Release your hold and be content with what you have. Let Me foster dependence in you. Separate yourself from all that interferes with My will for you.

Isaiah 55:9, Jeremiah 24:7, and Luke 9:23

# No Separation, No Darkness

You are moving in the direction of eternity and are closer than you were before. Your life is a part of eternity. If you will but see that closing your eyes in what the world calls death is merely the event that allows you to come alive in My presence! There is no separation, no darkness. You are on a continuum. I have promised to be with you always. Why would I leave you in that moment? You will feel My presence, My love, and My peace to a greater degree. Have faith, My sweet one.

Philippians 1:21 and Romans 8:38–39

# Your Future is in My Hands

The answers you seek are indeed in Me. I hold your future in My hands, therefore, your part is to walk it out--trusting and believing in Me. There can be no doubt of My goodness, even though your eyes cannot see what I see. You are meant to live day by day. When you focus on today all of your energy and faith is poured out in your present and not wasted on the past or your future. I fill you each day according to what I know you will need. As with the manna I provided for My people in the desert, you receive no more or less. Trust, in Me and My ability and willingness to provide for you, is built in this way.

Proverbs 27:1, Hebrews 11:1, and Exodus 16:4

# Set an Example

A rush of wind will blow away the cloud of darkness and confusion that has kept you trapped, unable to move forward. Breathe in My Spirit, feel the freedom, and taste the goodness of your Lord. Be free to follow Me in spirit and in truth. Loosen yourself from the ties that you think keep you bound, for in truth they have no power. You can walk free, but you choose to sit still. Where is the victory in that? If you stay seated, those who are watching you will not move either. You have power through your anointing. Your power is activated by movement, not by idleness. Take hold of what I have given you. Set an example that others can follow.

John 4:23, Isaiah 43:18–19, and James 2:24–26

# Step Out in Faith

Recall My gifts to you in times of need. Remind yourself of My goodness. You can do anything I ask of you. If I ask it of you, then I have put everything in place to equip you to do it, and your success is ensured. When you step out in faith, I honor your trust and commitment to Me. Your power is not in your flesh or your knowledge. Your power is supernatural and comes from My Holy Spirit. In the name of My Son, Jesus, you can do all things that I have ordained for you to do. I am with you at all times; therefore, you have continual access to Me. All power, all authority, all wisdom, and all knowledge are available to you to fulfill My purposes for you. Surrender all, My child.

I Thessalonians 5:24, Acts 1:8, John 15:16,
and I Chronicles 28:20

# The Purpose of Waiting

My ways cannot be known to you. My way is marked by obedience. Patience is necessary as you await My instruction, but My patient children are not idle, and waiting is not empty time. Life goes on, and time needs to be filled as you wait. Fill your time with what I have already instructed you to do. My words are not empty. All who wait on Me will be blessed by Me.

It is in the waiting that I do My work and you learn to be content and accept not knowing everything.

It is in the waiting that you are moved to seek My face and search for your answers in Me.

It is in the waiting that you seek My comfort, encouragement, and peace, and your endurance is built.

It is in the waiting, My sweet one, where you learn what faith is.

Isaiah 64:4, Colossians 1:11, Psalm 37:34, and Psalm 40:1

Fear

# My Words Are Your Strength

C all forth the army of God to defend My people. Do not let fear replace your faith in Me. My faithfulness is not in question. Renounce all that is not of Me. Pay close attention to My words. Study them and remember them in the moments you waver. My words will be your strength. You will find comfort and security when you adhere to them. Search out the meaning. Diligently seek out understanding.

2 Corinthians 5:10, Deuteronomy 7:9, and Psalm 138:3

# Walk in Freedom

Cast all your burdens on Me, for they are empty containers that give you the illusion of reality. I have removed all of the contents, and you are free. Walk in it, child. If you will look to Me for approval and inclusion, you will always find it. Allow Me to direct your path, and I will provide for your every need: physical, mental, emotional, and spiritual. Your family, friends, and work cannot fill up your bucket. I do that.

Psalm 55:22 and Proverbs 3:6

# Fear Is an Obstacle

Fear alone keeps you from becoming what I have planned for you. You hesitate and avoid obeying. What is the purpose? All is for naught if you do not move forward. Look into My eyes. Soak in them. What do you see there? Your destiny, your future, is in Me. Walk into it. The time for hesitation is over. Do not backtrack; there is nothing there. Be intent on Me. Look for Me in everything. Expect Me in all things. This ground is foreign to you. You have never been here with Me before. Rejoice! I have done a new thing in you! Let us run together the race I have laid out for you. We must move as one. Discover your true self in Me. You have come so far by My Spirit. Do not settle for less than I have for you. My hand is on your life—trust Me when I say this. Rejoice, My child! Lift up your head, for all is not lost. We have only begun, and My plan is in place.

Psalm 56:3, Proverbs 4:25–26, Joshua 1:9, and Isaiah 43:19

# Fear of Rejection

Meaningful interaction is uncomfortable for you. You have been deceived into believing that you could go through life alone. There is nothing wrong with taking time for yourself. It is healthy to enjoy time alone. But the enemy has created the illusion that time for yourself provides safety. When time for yourself is excessive, it becomes isolation. You try to walk alone and keep people on the periphery. You only reach out when you are in need of contact or if you feel them slipping away. You have a fear of being known and have not addressed the fear of rejection from which you are protecting yourself. You fear that if people know you they will see your flaws before you can speak them. If people know you, they will know your weaknesses, your secrets, and your shame, which you believe will then give them power over you. You are not an island for others to visit. The life I have for you requires more from you.

Hebrews 10:24–25, Hebrews 13:6, and Proverbs 29:25

# Hidden Thoughts

*L*oosen your hold on what you think gives you power—the power that comes from believing you are right. Examine what is at the bottom of your need to be right. Hold it up to My light. You will see it change before your eyes. Examine your thoughts and find the hidden ones. Those are the ones that direct you. Be on guard, for the enemy has knowledge of your weakness and need. He has entered into your thoughts and maintains a presence. I have not left you. Proceed according to My voice. You are fear driven, even though My Word says, "I have not given you a spirit of fear, but one of power, love, and a sound mind."

Proverbs 21:2, 1 John 1:7–9, and 2 Timothy 1:7

# Do Not Be Afraid

oldly face the future. Your fear and your flesh propel you away from Me, which is the devil's plan for you. But your answer lies with Me. Winnow each issue to the core; and trust My wisdom, not your own. Put your hand in Mine and your faith in Me, for My strength is transferred in this manner. Do not be afraid of what you see. The devil casts an image that is only an illusion. If you are focused on Me, you will not be fooled by his artistry, for your eyes will see the truth and you will not be deceived. You are moving forward and cannot be held back by force, only by ignorance. You cannot know Me if you don't know My Word. I am My Word.

Psalm 34:4, Romans 11:33, and 2 Corinthians 4:4

# Savor My Words

ou will always know My voice. Never fear, for I am with you. Come to Me, My child. Lay your head on My shoulder. I am your comfort, your Father in Heaven. My words have power. Use them wisely. Do not throw them out like stones, but savor them as food. Do not worry about tomorrow, for tomorrow will take care of itself. Today is Mine. Do today what I ask of you. Do not wait, for you must act quickly. Speak when I tell you to speak. Listen when I tell you to listen. Act when I tell you to act, for I am your God. There is no one like Me.

Isaiah 41:10, Matthew 28:20, Matthew 6:34, and Jeremiah 7:23

# Focus

# Put Me First

Pick out a place in your home where we will meet, and make it your own. Narrow your field of vision to focus on what I have put before you. All else is a distraction and will not lead where I want you to go. Manage your time to include Me so that I am most important to you. When you put Me first, all else falls away or falls into place. Failure to do so leaves your mind and your life cluttered. Be on guard, for when I am not first, the enemy gains entrance. Make sure that your heart is free, unencumbered, and ready to receive. Let Me pour into you today what I know you will need for your journey. Let Me fill you with My Spirit until you overflow with My fruit. Call upon Me, sweet one, and wait for My answer.

Know that My goodness accompanies My answer.

Know that My faithfulness ensures My answer.

Know that My love endures in My answer.

Know that My will empowers My answer.

Need causes you to ask. Hope anticipates My answer. Faith allows you to wait. It is in the waiting that your faith grows.

Matthew 6:6, Psalm 119:68, Numbers 23:19,
1 Corinthians 13:8, and Hebrews 13:20–21

# Plan Wisely

Carefully plan your path. My Spirit will guide you in those moments when you lose focus. We meet at the well, child. You drink of My Living Water; therefore, you have what you need to continue. Speak out to those who have ears to hear. I have much to say. Do not get ahead of yourself. My army is in place. Be encouraged by My Word. Acknowledge Me in all you do.

Luke 14:28 and John 4:14

# Distractions Change Focus

Take heed, My child, to stay close and listen carefully to Me. My warnings are out of love for you. The way can be treacherous without instruction. It is good for you to see how slippery the slope can become when you look away from Me. When you allow distractions to gain your attention, you lose your focus on Me and what I am doing. You forget who I am and begin to focus on our enemy and what man can do. Your fears are unfounded. Do not be afraid of the unknown, and do not be afraid of the known, for I am with you always. My Word promises that, and I am My Word. Temporary discomfort or loss of face is unimportant in My plan. My purpose in you and for you will lead you when you come to places that are unfamiliar. You cannot allow your feelings and thoughts to hold you back or change your direction. Call on Me in all things; I listen for you always. Let nothing stand in your way. All hope is found in Me; therefore, place yours in Me. Believe in Me. Come to Me. Fear no evil, for I am with you.

Proverbs 8:33–34, Mark 4:19, Deuteronomy 31:6, and James 1:2–4

# Today Is Your Day

Focus on what I have put before you. Block out the unnecessary. Detach from the unimportant. Present yourself to Me as a clean vessel, prepared to hold what I have to pour into you. Do not fail to recognize My will for you in this. Open yourself up to My Spirit. Hear Me as I speak My heart and mind to you. Be not afraid of tomorrow. Tomorrow is Mine, and all that it holds has already been ordained by Me. Seek only to know My will for today. You cannot operate in your tomorrows. Today is your day, a gift from Me. Behold My Glory today. Anticipate tomorrow, but do not dwell there. You lose sight of what I have given you in today when tomorrow is your focus.

Luke 10:41–42, Isaiah 30:21, and Matthew 6:31–34

# Do Not Lose Focus

Let us walk awhile together. Take My hand and listen closely to My words. You are not always aware of My presence. Seeing Me in all your moments is important. You lose sight of Me when you begin to focus on what's going on around you. When people or circumstances gain your attention, your thoughts and emotions become disconnected from My presence and you lose My peace. My peace is part of My presence, and therefore it is always available for you. Pay attention to what you focus on as you move through your day. Make note of the times you become distracted and lose focus. You will see a pattern emerge. Apply this information to gain better control over your thoughts and thus reclaim My peace. Make sure you portion out your time each day to include Me.

Psalm 119:33–35, Mark 4:19, Isaiah 26:3, and
2 Corinthians 10:5

# Capture Your Thoughts

Forego your pleasures for Me today. Take pleasure in Me, your loving Father. I am the Living God who makes all things possible. Focus on Me. I am all that you need. When you can get yourself out of your thoughts, you will see Me. As you focus more on Me, you will become less concerned with yourself or how others see you. You will be known to all as one who loves Me. Narrow your gaze and capture your thoughts. Do not focus on the world and all it has to offer. Fortunes are made and lost, but My rewards are eternal. Evaluate your desire for more. Take stock of your possessions and depend on Me to provide daily.

Mark 10:21, Psalm 16:5, 2 Corinthians 10:5, and Psalm 145:15–16

# Refine Your Gaze

*I* am all that you need. When you can get yourself out of your thoughts, you will see Me. As you focus more on Me, you will become less concerned with yourself, the cares of life, and how others see you. Cast all doubt into the sea. You are well prepared for the coming season. As you refine your gaze, your focus will shift from internal to external, and we will be on the same page. Taking your eyes off yourself will free you up to see what I need you to see. You are not unimportant, and I am taking care of you. My grace and My provision are enough for you. Labor in the fields of others, because we are working in the fallow fields of My people.

Philippians 2:3–4, 2 Corinthians 5:5, and I John 3:17–18

# Staying Focused

Listen, My child! You are weary of striving toward an unreachable goal, one that isn't in my plan for you. Your hands work at staying busy with things that are not of Me. These are things that occupy your mind but do not reach your heart. You are wasting time instead of using that valuable commodity for My purposes. You choose to distract yourself with other things instead of purposing your heart to accomplish what needs to be done. Productivity is vital when you are moving down My path for you. Do not check out; it stops growth and forward movement. Check in with Me for counsel and direction. Your time is a gift from Me. Use it wisely.

Luke 10:41–42, Jeremiah 10:23, and Psalm 16:7

# Fruit

# Bear Fruit

You are right to call on Me, for all power is held in My name for you. There is none but Me who will provide for you in that perfect way. Look to Me, believe in Me, and trust Me. I am good to you in all things. All you need is in Me, so let Me have My way in you and you will bear sweet, delicious fruit. Your fruit will bear fruit, and My vineyard will grow and expand! Rely on Me to cultivate the ground through you. I will use you to prune, to water, and to fertilize the ground. You are my laborer. My vineyard awaits your hands. The harvest will be great, and My kingdom will reap the fruit of the harvest.

Jeremiah 10:6, Psalm 16:5–6, and Colossians 1:10

# Fruitfulness

Fallow fields abound. Carefully plan your day. Catch hold of all that I have for you. My mission is being accomplished through you. Your work is anointed by Me to produce the fruit I have ordained for you. Marry yourself to the concept of fruitfulness. When one is married, a commitment is made to be faithful—to work at and nurture the relationship. To be fruitful, it is also necessary to faithfully work and nurture the ground where seeds have been planted. Produce fruit, My child, by becoming a laborer in the fallow fields of My people. Never give up or grow weary; for remember, I am your strength. I provide all you need to work My fields. You lack nothing but desire. Come out of yourself and look toward others. Ask Me for revelation and discernment. I will show you the need and equip you to provide for that need. Make the most of your time.

Hosea 10:12, Titus 3:14, Galatians 6:9, Hebrews 13:21

# Good Fruit

Honor Me with your heart and lips. Prepare for Me a harvest of fruit. Instant meals are not possible in My kingdom. The fruit I seek is gathered after much preparation. Cultivating the soil, planting the seeds, watering the ground, and fertilizing are necessary. Pruning and training a vine refines the plant and equips it to produce good fruit in abundance. You yourself are good fruit, prepared by others, pruned and refined by My hand. Take heart as you hear My voice. Your ears will tingle, and your heart beat with the joy known only to those who seek Me and find Me.

Psalm 86:12, 1 Corinthians 3:6—9, and John 15:1—3

# Pour Yourself Out

Continue to pour yourself into My people. Your cup will never go empty when dipped into My well. As long as you continue to seek Me, you will be filled. I do not hide from those who seek, but many search with eyes that do not see. I stand in the midst of their circumstances, but they are blinded to My presence. They do not recognize Me because they don't know Me. Lead My people to Me. Pour yourself out, My child. You will reap the fruit of your labor.

John 4:13, Matthew 13:15, and Isaiah 58:9–11

# Produce Good Fruit

Measure it all as joy. My gift to you is the fullness of being. Count on Me to deliver what I have promised. There is more to come. Wait on Me as I move in the lives of others, those who have been chosen to partake in the goodness of the Lord. All are invited, but not all will come, although My table seats many. Measure your worth and value according to My definition of you. Others cannot see you as I do, so they define you out of their own ignorance. Be careful that you do not define others. See them as I see them so you will treat them with grace and love. Produce good fruit by your willingness to do this. How you treat others bears witness to My presence in you. Take hold of this truth as you go through your day. Be on guard for wayward thoughts and spontaneous words, for a sweet smile that covers up a wicked heart is deceitful. Pour yourself out on those who are parched and weary. Be the lifter of their heads so their eyes will look up and see Me. Point them in the right direction so they will find Me. Do for others what was done for you.

Ephesians 3:19, Matthew 22:14, and Isaiah 41:17

# Raise Your Banner

There is more to do. You are not yet finished with what I have for you. Pay no attention to the words of others, for they may distract or discourage you. Pay close attention to My words, because they will inform you of My will for you. Meaning is procured from research. Interpretation comes after deliberation. Success evolves when you are diligent in your efforts. Therefore, study My word diligently for meaning and application in your life. You will produce fruit in this manner, and your fruit will be your banner. Banners are raised in announcement; banners are raised in battle; banners are raised in victory. Produce fruit so that you can raise your banner in victory and bring glory to My name.

Ephesians 2:10, Acts 4:19, Joshua 1:8, and Jeremiah 51:27

# Reap What You Sow

Listen to Me, My child. Prepare the way of the Lord, for it is I who will come in glory! The fields are ready to be plowed, and you will reap what you sow. Therefore, be aware of what you are sowing. I have placed you in fertile fields, and the ground is ready for planting. Take advantage of this time to sow your seed. The seeds you plant will produce fruit. You decide—by your manner, words, tone, and actions—what type of fruit will be produced. Speak the words that bring life and renew others' spirits. I am watching. Represent Me well!

Psalm 24:7–10, Galatians 6:7–8, and Matthew 12:33

God Has a Plan

# Captured Heart

*I* will capture your heart with My words. They will come on the wind, and you will abide in them. Pronounce a decree of My love for you, since there is a question in your mind of its certainty. Place your hand in Mine as we move into your destiny. Hold fast to what I have put in you. Do not mistake silence for anger or stillness for disapproval. My plan is still in place and has an appointed time for fruition. Rejoice at the sound of My name spoken by the prophets, and call on My glory to descend as a covering.

Psalm 104:4, Job 22:28, Hebrews 10:23 and Exodus 13:21

# I Planned for You

Call on Me. Come to Me where I can be found. I am near and ready to listen. I see you and long to embrace you. Trust Me and let Me show My love to you as I have always wanted. Let Me be your God. I call you by name; call Me by Mine. I am Yahweh, Lord, and I am Father. You are My sweet, sweet child. I have known you since before time began. I planned for you. I awaited your birth because you are part of My plans. They are good because I am good. Each journey is unique, but they all lead to Me. Come—walk with Me. Follow Me; I know the way, so let Me lead. When you take the first step, My Spirit will carry you forward.

Psalm 145:18, Isaiah 63:16, and Jeremiah 29:11

# The Perfect Fit

I will summon My people to Me, for where I go, you will go. I will never leave you or forsake you. Forget what is behind and press on to what is before you. Place your hand in Mine, and you will see how Mine covers yours completely. All that you are, every aspect of your life, is important to Me. I do not reject any part of it. Work with Me as I mold you. For I know what it is that I do. The shape we are achieving is a perfect fit for the plan I have prepared for you. Rejoice in Me, for I am God Almighty! Make all effort to follow Me. Marshal your defenses, for the devil seeks entry. Pay close attention.

Genesis 28:15, Philippians 3:13–14, Matthew 10:29–31, and Ephesians 6:10–18

# Do Not Compare

My hand covers the work I have given you to do. Stay close to Me so I can instruct you in the way you should go. Do not compare yourself with others. Let them be who I have ordained for them to be. Stand alone in the place I have designed for you. It fits only you, as theirs fit only them. Value My instructions. Become diligent in all you do. Move past what you think and what you want in order to hear what I think and what I want for you. Move through your feelings and choose action. Begin to exercise the self-control muscle that I have given you. Harken unto Me, child. I love you with a father's love.

Ephesians 2:10, Psalm 32:8, and Galatians 6:4

# Let Me Prune You

You are complete and whole. Do not wear your inadequacies as a cloak. They are not meant to cover you and weigh you down. They are a small part of the complete you. Your weaknesses are lightweight. They are part of the many layers of your personality and character. Let Me decide where to prune. Do not be dismayed at what I leave in you. I know exactly how to use every aspect of your being for My purpose and for My glory. Rejoice that I am aware of all that you are, and all that you are is completely accepted and loved by Me.

2 Corinthians 12:9, John 15:2,
Ephesians 1:11–12, and Romans 15:7

# Divine Perspective

Stay mindful, alert, and aware. There is an enemy who constantly seeks to destroy you. Be on guard for those moments when things happen suddenly and without warning. Know that suddenly is not a part of My vocabulary. It is a concept of your human perspective. Therefore, the divine perspective takes authority over the human. When we are in fellowship and close communion, your access to Me and all that I am is assured. My plan for you includes these moments. Turn to Me and trust Me to have the answers and solutions to every situation or circumstance in which you suddenly find yourself. Have confidence in My foreknowledge of it and My promise to give you a hope and a future. Fix your eyes on Me. Make your ears keen to hear My voice and open your heart to My Word. This is the way you will renew your mind.

I Peter 5:8, Jeremiah 29:11, and Matthew 13:16–17

# Follow My Plan

I speak My heart and mind to you as you seek Me. Forego your pleasures for time spent with Me. The value of My words and My presence far outweighs any benefits gained from other pursuits. You are My own, bought with a price; you are important to Me. Call on Me for your heart's desires, for I am listening intently. Be mindful of all I have called on you to accomplish for My kingdom. The work I have prepared for you to do is before you. Move forward with My Spirit; you can count on Me to direct you. Be mindful of My presence throughout the day, seeking Me and searching for Me in all you do. I am always near. Listen for Me: I will instruct you and guide you, for I have a plan for your life and a plan for this day. If you follow My plan each day, then My plan for your life will be achieved in a timely manner. Rejoice in this and have hope in My words. Depend on Me to do this in you.

Psalm 16:11, Psalm 25:12, and Proverbs 19:21

# Eternal Life

Eternal life exists in the present and doesn't begin when you die. You were born with an eternal soul and became a part of eternity at birth. So let go of all preconceived ideas and beliefs. They limit your thinking and restrict your growth. Be open to the leading of My Holy Spirit, for He knows My heart and mind. Therefore, He knows what I have for you, and He has a way for you to attain it.

John 17:3 and 1 Corinthians 2:10–11

# Surrender Your Pleasures

Blessings upon you, My child. Entertain no thought of failure. That is not possible when I am involved. Truly I say unto you, forego your pleasures for My plan. You will reap the benefits of abstaining from those things that bring you momentary pleasure. Come to Me when you are tempted. I have your answer. Do not avoid Me, but seek Me out, for I will strengthen you. I will inhabit the moment with you, and it will pass. When you immediately seek Me, none that the devil sends on assignment will succeed. Guard your heart and mind with My strength and wisdom. He uses your weaknesses to attack, and when you are not focused on Me, he gains entrance.

Titus 2:11–13, 1 Corinthians 10:13, and Psalm 105:4

# I Sustain You

Rejoice as you move through your days with ease and grace. Forfeit your time to Me and allow Me to arrange it according to My purposes and plans for you. We have many miles to go, but I will sustain you along the way. Take heart that I have a plan in place, for it relieves you of responsibility to all but Me. For to whom should you look for truth, wisdom, and guidance other than the One who spoke all into existence?

Proverbs 20:24, Galatians 6:5, and Amos 4:13

# My Plan Requires Movement

My plans for you require movement from you. Do not be static. Stationary objects get run over or passed by. There is danger in that. Complacency and ambivalence are not your friends. Focus and direction will lead you where you need to go. Ask for these things, and you will have them. I have an unending supply of all you need, for I am God. I am the One who provides My children with everything that is needed to fulfill My plan for them and everything they want according to My will for them. Are you one of My own? Let Me supply your need. Just ask, and I will provide.

Proverbs 12:24, Luke 12:31, and 1 John 5:14–15

# Invite Me In

Personal opinions do not matter in My kingdom. Only My voice in your ear is important. Only My Spirit moving in your life is essential to your well-being. Release to Me your thoughts, ideas, and feelings so there will be room for all I have for you. Your life becomes too crowded and noisy when you try to hold on to what you want while you also ask what I have for you. My people plan their way without a thought of Me. I come into focus when you are challenged by adversity or painful results from poor planning. I can certainly fix your mistakes, but I am the Creator. Let Me show you the plan I have created for your life. We have to be in agreement for you to walk out My plan for you. We cannot agree if I am not involved in the conversation. Invite Me in.

Deuteronomy 5:23, James 4:13–15, Genesis 16:2, and Kings 23:3

# The Tapestry of Life

Pieces of time are strung together to form the threads of your life. They don't appear to connect, but I have ordered the timing of each one, and the tapestry I am weaving is known only to Me. Do not question your past or your present. Do not speculate about your future. Trust Me with all. I am using your past to imprint your present and future. Trust Me to be who I say I am, for in My hands, all of your hours and all of your moments will be fashioned into My perfect plan for you. You can only see the underside of your tapestry—seemingly broken and disjointed threads with no continuity or direction or beauty. But I see the beauty of the finished life—woven by My hands with love—using the perfect colors and form. I love you, My child. Trust Me that life seen from your side of the tapestry does not resemble the perfection of My work in you.

Isaiah 14:24, Jeremiah 29:11–14, and Philippians 1:6

# Walk with Me

Place your hand in Mine, for you have all you need in Me. Walk with Me into your future so that all of your days unfold according to My plan for you. When you let go of Me, the enemy has an opening and an opportunity to lead you in the wrong direction. Stay close to Me!

Deuteronomy 5:33 and 2 Corinthians 2:11

# God's Power

# Christ's Authority

s the flowers bloom to announce the change of season, you are seeing the first blossoms of the fruit you have labored for in My vineyard. Tend My garden; plow My fields. I am harvesting My fruit through you, not because of you. Wishing and hoping can produce nothing. Faith in Me and My ability to perform My Word is what you need. If I say it, it happens. You'll hear no other voice that speaks with My authority. Heed My words. Listen for Me and watch Me move.

Deuteronomy 11:14, Jeremiah 1:12, and Matthew 28:18

# Glorify Me

o everything in My name and for My glory! I will be glorified in all the earth! Awaken, you sleeper, for salvation is at hand. The salvation of the Lord draws near. Do not be afraid. Fear is your enemy. Have faith in Me, the One who saves. Call forth the army of the Lord! We are many. I am the King and the Great I Am! Bow down before Me in worship and praise. I lead, and you must follow, for I know the way. Trust in Me. I am your Father in Heaven and know My purposes for you. As I reveal your sins to you, do not be ashamed. It is necessary to purify you. We are at war, and My warriors must be clean and ready to fight with My weapons of righteousness and holiness. Be holy as I am holy. I will come in like a flood, overtaking everything, and raise My banner. Do not deny Me this pleasure. I am doing a work in you. You are one of My own, and I will perform My will in you. Allow My Spirit free rein in your heart. Give yourself over to My will for you, for it is good and will prosper you in all you do. Remember My promises, child.

Stand on My Word. It is your foundation and starting point.
Learn My Word so that it becomes your words. I am in My Word,
and I seek to perform it.

Joel 2:11, Daniel 11:35, Isaiah 59:19–20, and Jeremiah 1:12

# An Immovable Force

Drink till you are full of the goodness of the Lord. Pass the cup to those who are thirsty, for there is plenty for all. Seek Me and you will find Me. If you do not seek Me, you will go dry, and what I ask of you will seem overwhelming. Be aware of your weaknesses and depend on Me so that the battle the devil wages will be against an immovable force. It is true that in your weakness I am strong. As long as you come to Me in your weakness and acknowledge it to Me, I will win the battle. I am the Immovable Force that will overcome the enemy, and you will lift your voice in praise.

Luke 11:9–10, 2 Corinthians 12:9–10, and Psalm 18:2

# I Am Your Source

You are My child, and I take care of My own! There is no power in Heaven or on Earth that can stand against Me, for I am God the Almighty! Call on Me when you are in need. It is My joy to rescue you and fulfill your needs. Heaven rejoices at the sound of My name: Yahweh, Lord of All, King, and Redeemer! Rejoice in Me. Rejoice at the sound of My name, for your power emanates from Me, the Source.

1 John 4:4, Psalm 91:14–15, and Psalm 66:1–3

# My Strength in Your Weakness

My blessings will be upon you as you seek direction and instruction. Do you see how I use what you consider a weakness to exhibit My strength in you? I use your weakness as a vessel to move in and through you. When you respond to instruction and are willing to follow the direction of My Holy Spirit, you are submitting to My will, and therefore I become strong in you.

Proverbs 8:17 and Isaiah 40:29–31

# Prepare Your Heart

ountains have crumbled at the sound of My name.
Demons flee, and the righteous rejoice. I am Jesus,
Savior, the Holy One of Israel. Prepare your heart
to receive all I have for you. There is a great bounty on the horizon, and it requires an open heart and willing spirit to receive
it. Be forewarned that the nature of My gift will not resemble the
packages you are used to receiving, but it will bring joy none-
theless. Present yourself to Me as a clean vessel, emptied of all
but Me. Make the most of your days because time is short. I am
arising from My throne, and it causes change; the stirring in My
chamber produces profound changes in the world. The enemy
has stepped up his attack, and I am responding to the cry of My
people. Be secure in the knowledge that I am moving.

Psalm 46:2, 2 Timothy 2:21, and Psalm 7:6

# Weakness Is Not a Detriment

Do not be ashamed of your weakness, for your weakness is the way I gain access to you. The strong do not seek Me because they do not believe they need Me. It is the weak who search for Me and cry out to Me. Therefore, rejoice in your weakness! It is the open door to My power in you.

1 Samuel 2:9 and Psalm 61:2–3

# My Voice Carries

D o not doubt My love for you. Troubles come and go, but My love is forever. My Glory will shine for all to see. My time is coming soon, so be ready to take your place in My army of righteousness. We are marching toward our appointed destiny. I am with you at every step. My voice speaks clearly to those who are listening. March with Me, My children, for the battle rages on all sides, but with Me, there is safety and protection. My words are spoken to those with ears to hear. My voice is carried across the land by those who listen for Me and to Me. I have made you for this time. I honor your obedience. It is a time of renewal and revival! My Glory will be revealed to all who seek Me. Continue to seek Me at all times and in all things. Seasons change, and you are in a new season. Rejoice! Lift the banner high! Raise your voices to the heavens. The sound is sweet to My ears.

Isaiah 60:19, Psalm 85:6, and Psalm 20:5

*God's Word*

# Cast Aside Your Treasures

ow down before Me as you worship. Make your ears keen to listen to Me. You, who have nothing without Me, must give all to Me. Count up your treasures and then cast them aside, for they are nothing in comparison with the treasure I have stored up for you in Heaven. Hold fast to My truths. Base your life on My Word. Listen closely when I speak. For My Word and My very self are your true treasures.

Matthew 13:44 and Colossians 3:16–17

# Unchanging

Carbon copies are never as clear as the original. Reproductions can be identified on close examination. Examine Me, My children, and see if I am not who I say I am—the Alpha and the Omega. Search Me out. Test Me! Try Me and see who your God is. My Word stands alone: breathed by My Spirit, written by man, and gathered into a book of truth that has remained unchanged and unaltered. My Word cannot be altered or changed in any way because I am My Word. I am unchanging—the same yesterday, today, and tomorrow. Refresh yourself with My Word. It holds all your answers and My will for you.

Revelation 1:8, 2 Timothy 3:16-17, and John 1:1

# The Word Sustains

old fast to My truth. It is your lifeblood and nourishment for your soul. You are fed by My words, which speak to your heart. My Word will sustain all who desire Me. The hungry shall eat, and the thirsty shall drink their fill. I am the Living Water who will quench the thirst of all who drink. Come satisfy yourself in Me. Your heart is what I seek. Open it up to Me so that I can make it Mine

Proverbs 2:6, Isaiah 55:2, and John 7:37

# Motion Sickness

otion sickness comes to those who are battered about by the circumstances of their lives. I offer a safe port in their storms, a protected cove of peaceful waters. Some storms can be viewed from a distance, and that makes preparation simple. But many times, storms arise unexpectedly and require immediate response. Hasty preparation leaves gaps and holes, but action based on a firm foundation is solid and complete, providing confidence and protection for those who are prepared. To prepare well, build a repertoire of My words—they will defeat the enemy in your heart and strengthen the hearts and minds of all who hear.

Psalm 107:28–29, James 1:6, and Matthew 7:24–27

# Prepare for Enemy Attack

My hand covers you, My Word teaches you, and My Spirit leads you, so faint not at the attack of the enemy. His moves are bold, but the results are weak when you are prepared in Me. He gains no ground in well-cultivated soil. Good ground produces good fruit. Refresh yourself with My Word. It holds all of your answers and My will for you.

Psalm 20:6, Romans 8:14, and John 15:16

# Search My Word

I will pour forth My Spirit on all who call on Me. Wise men encounter problems and immediately seek My face. Foolish men encounter problems and ask the world for its answer. Where do you look when you seek a solution? My Word says that I give wisdom to anyone who asks for it, and I give without judgment. Why then would you hesitate to ask for what you need or seek it elsewhere? The foolish can become wise if they turn in My direction. Your wisdom comes from Me and not from the books you read or the seminars you attend. Seek Me out; search My Word for information, instruction, guidance, and evidence of My love for you. You are My Beloved. I withhold nothing from you that you need and fulfill your desires in accordance with My will for you. Therefore, find all that you seek and everything you search for in My Word.

I Corinthians 3:19, James 1:5, and Philippians 4:19

# Spiritual Awakening

Spiritual awakening is taking place within you. Nurture your spirit. Feed it the only food that nourishes—My Word. Read My Word and find your daily bread there. Remember, I am My Word; therefore, the more you eat of it, the more of Me is in you. It is what you have asked for. Since you reap what you sow, plant carefully, child. Be sure of the seeds you sow so that you can be certain of what you will harvest. The time invested in My Word will be of more benefit to you than any other type of investment you make. You are prepared for this season. Don't hold back. Give your all to Me, as I have given My all for you.

Ephesians 5:14, Matthew 4:4, and Galatians 6:7

# The Word as Wind

My Word goes forth as the wind. The wind is felt but not seen. It permeates the cracks and crevices of all things. It enters even when doors are closed and walls are present. My Word enters into your heart and mind just as the wind enters into the structures of this world. It is an inexorable force—relentless, not to be stopped or changed. Remember, I am My Word! Therefore, seek Me. Search out My Word. Open your heart and mind to My Word as though you are opening the doors of your home and letting the wind blow through—cleansing and refreshing your spaces. It blows away dust and debris. When your mind is closed and your heart is hidden and dark, the air around you becomes heavy and dank, wet and cold in an unpleasant way. Just as the wind pushes the storm clouds away and allows the sun to shine, My Word pushes the darkness from your mind and allows My light to shine.

Hebrews 4:12, Psalm 119:10–11, and Psalm 19:7–11

# Guard Your Tongue

# Be on Guard

Call on Me, child. I will deliver on My promises! I am the King. Serve Me well, faithful one. One way you do this is by being on guard, for the enemy is watching and waiting for an opening. Do not give him one. Guard your tongue. Measure your words. Be careful as you speak, and count on Me. I am with you always. I am your rearguard. I will keep you safe as long as you lean into Me, so trust Me in this, little one. You are Mine, and I cover My own. Tiny words produce big results. Your words do not have to be big, with many letters, to bring results. Choose your words wisely so you can be understood by those who are listening.

Proverbs 21:23, Isaiah 52:12, and Colossians 4:6

# Discord Does Not Honor Me

Make a way for the Lord to enter into the hearts and minds of His people, for it is only through salvation that My people will enjoy My presence forever. Make My coming known to all. Persevere in your efforts, for My kingdom awaits the answer. As you persevere, remember: peace and unity are mighty swords with which to fight the enemy. Discord does not honor Me. Make every effort to live in peace with those around you. Hold back the words that separate and harm. Speak only those words that bring unity. Harbor no ill will against anyone. It weakens you. Throw off all offense as a dirty rag. Do not fear this process, for it is My will for you. Rejoice, for I am coming soon. You will see the glory of the Lord in the land of the living. Rejoice!

1 John 5:11–13, Ephesians 4:3, Leviticus 19:18,
and Proverbs 19:11

# Do Not Be Fooled

Some things are not what they seem. Certain people have hidden agendas and will present themselves in a way that is pleasing. Do not be fooled. Always be cautious when talking to others. Speak My truth, and say only what is necessary. Rely not on your own understanding of events, but seek Me for the interpretation. Resist the urge to define and explain, but pause as you wait for My Spirit of discernment. This is about trusting in My leading, recognizing My voice, and heeding it in a timely manner. I know your weaknesses and your strengths. I am making you strong in Me. It is important that you learn to discern spirits, which requires being alert and aware at all times. This will only happen when you are completely attuned to My voice. Listen for Me; I will speak to you at all times. My instructions will be clear, and obedience is necessary. This is how we walk together. I lead, you follow. I speak, you obey. You will be blessed through this.

Matthew 7:15–16, Proverbs 3:5, and Proverbs 2:1–5

# Measure Your Words

There is much work to do. When you open your mouth and let the River of Living Water pour out of you, I will pour forth My Spirit onto My people to bless them with correction, encouragement, and comfort. Let Me burn the chaff. Once I have pruned what is unnecessary, a solid core of faith will remain. Honor Me in all you do. I have set you aside for My purposes. Manifested in love, you were formed by My hand. Produce fruit for Me. Continue to till My garden with the tools I have given you and do not rely on your own understanding. Be prepared to measure your words. They have power and purpose. Do not speak lightly and without thought. That can be damaging. Pray and seek Me for your words, for then you will be heard, and no misunderstanding will interfere with My purpose.

John 7:38, Matthew 3:12, Psalm 119:73, and Proverbs 12:18

# Hearing God

# Come into Agreement

orego all your pleasures for Me. Listen to Me and only Me. Your protection is complete. Satisfy yourself at My feet. Make known to Me your requests, for I listen intently to you. I bless you, My child, for you are after My heart. Seek My wisdom in all things and come into agreement with Me, for I have a way for you to go. Territories will be conquered in this process. Areas that have been blocked will be opened, and all blessings from heaven shall flow down upon those who follow this path.

Psalm 5:11–12 and Psalm 25:10

# I Cannot Be Surprised

I am here with you, My precious child. I hear your prayers because I listen intently to you. Nothing escapes me. Come close. I am the Holy One! Bow down before Me in reverence and worship Me in My temple. Hold on to Me as I move forward. Focus on the issues I put before you. Listen, so you do not misunderstand My words. I will pour out My Spirit on all who partake! My glory will be evident in the homes of My people. I am more than able to circumvent the enemy because I know everything. I cannot be surprised. Remain in Me and do not worry. Listen to My words and remember them, for I have much to say today. Call My name in times of trouble; I am always near. I will come in like a flood to wash away the enemy—he has no foothold here in you. Trust My words. Seek Me every day, in all things, and I will direct your path.

Hebrews 4:13, Psalm 5:7, Acts 2:17–18, and Proverbs 2:1–5

# Adapt Your Ears

My Word goes forth in the land. My voice can be heard, but ears are not open to it. Adapt your ears to hear My voice. Can you not detect it? My voice whispers, but it also crashes like the waves of the ocean; it soothes like a mother soothes her child. It is in the wind that blows softly through the trees; it is also in the force of the gale that lifts and separates. Listen to My voice! I need to be heard. My Spirit seeks those who seek Me. Listen for Me in all things and in all situations. I speak continually, but no one hears. You hear what you want to hear at times. You need the will to do what is foreign or uncomfortable for you. Challenges in life will come and go, but I remain the same.

Proverbs 3:6, Proverbs 8:17, and Psalm 29:3–9

# Heed My Words

Call on Me, for I am here. There is nothing that I cannot or will not do in you. My plans are good and perfect. Lean on Me in times of trouble. Be on guard, for the enemy watches for an opening. Listen for My instructions. Be sensitive to My Spirit; I will lead you down right paths, away from the enemy's traps. Acknowledge Me in all your ways. All that you do is under My scrutiny. I examine all efforts for purpose and motive. Do not be afraid of that, but rejoice in it. My refining fire is fresh and produces a new person. Welcome Me and My instruction. Heed My words and respond accordingly, for they will bring you life.

Jeremiah 29:11, Isaiah 58:11, Psalm 66:10–12

# Listen Intently

Words are inadequate but useful in speaking to you. I use words that are understood by you, but they cannot convey My true thoughts. My thoughts and ways are so much higher than yours that they are unexplainable. So I made it simpler for you, because you need to hear Me. My wisdom has come at great cost, but the payment has been made in full. My Son, Jesus, whom I love, was sacrificed for you. Honor Him. Obey Him. Love Him. He is My only begotten Son. You were adopted into My family, and you are My own. My plans have always included you. I didn't have to call you; I wanted to. Rejoice in this truth! Hold on to Me through these times. Never lose sight of Me. Those who stray can become lost and confused. I am moving in one direction. Move with Me. Stay close so that you can detect My movement. Listen intently for My instruction, for My will is revealed through it.

Isaiah 55:8, Ephesians 1:5, and Colossians 2:18–19

# Open Your Heart and Mind

Behold! My glory rests upon you. I will anoint you to hear Me, to receive My Spirit, and to bathe in My light. Come to Me, My child. Hear My words as I speak them. Open your heart and mind to Me and let Me have My way in you. My desire is to be close to you and draw you near. Get to know Me and let Me define Myself to you so there is no misconception or mistaken belief about My goodness, mercy, or My love for you. I am God, your loving Father in Heaven.

1 Peter 4:14, Psalm 65:4, and Ephesians 2:4

# Pray for Hearing

eek Me for Me, and I will be found by you! Call on Me in times of trouble, and your answer will come. Hold on to Me, for My cloak is large and covers all who choose Me. My words are true and have meaning for those who hear, so pray for hearing. I will not shout—for I do not have to. Expect Me to speak, for I yearn to speak to My people. They have forgotten the sound of My voice because they are distracted by the many voices of the world. The enemy speaks in many tongues and through many portals—portals that humanity has opened and that didn't come from Me. Be on guard, for the enemy's tongue is smooth and speaks the promises for which all ears yearn. Learn his ways, compare them with Mine, and choose. You will know the enemy and those who are his by their fruit.

Mark 4:19, Daniel 8:25, and Matthew 7:15–16

# Be Cautious and Watchful

Come to Me for your answers. I am near and listening. When you surrender to Me and let Me have My way in you, then you can learn to know My voice. My truth is your truth. Do not let the enemy play tricks on you and bring confusion. I will always alert you to his schemes. Rest easy, but be cautious and watchful. Do not allow fear to enter into your thinking. It will derail your progress.

Psalm 62:8 and Luke 21:34–36

You are Called to Labor

# Broken Vessels

arbor no ill will toward others. This is not the time to allow unforgiveness to lead you away from the task at hand. Remain in Me and allow Me to heal and bind your wounds. All of your tomorrows are in My hands. You are a broken vessel, which allows My blessings to flow through you to others. Rejoice in that! If you are not broken, I cannot use you. A perfect vessel has no cracks or holes, and therefore, My goodness, My grace, My essence cannot seep through it and touch another. So do not consider your pain something to avoid, but rather as an opportunity for Me to heal and smooth the jagged edges of the wound. And through this opening, I will pour more of Myself out onto those who need Me.

Ephesians 4:31–32, Psalm 147:3, and 2 Corinthians 1:4–6

# Make a Way

The peace that surpasses all understanding is yours. Rest in it. Make a way in the desert for Me. Clear out whatever obstructs the flow of the movement of My Spirit in you. My path to others goes through you. I use you to touch others, just as I used others to touch you. Each one in turn gives Me access to another. I am the Vine, and you are the branches. My desire is to nourish My people, and through you, to touch those I am calling to be Mine.

Philippians 4:7, Matthew 5:14–16, and John 15:5

# Divine Order

Cast out all doubt, for your prayer has been heard. I am more than equal to the task. Therefore, it shall be done in you as you ask. Prayers are a power source for My people, unique to My beloved. Make a joyful noise! Prepare the way for Me to enter into the hearts and minds of My people. Lay before Me the appropriate robes that I may walk into their lives. I gain entrance through you and others like you. It is the order I put in place before time began. You have come after others, and others will come after you. It is your willingness to partake and participate in this divine order that grows My kingdom. I have ordained for you all to know one another in Heaven. No one will be a stranger to the others. It is not possible for you to understand the number of people you have touched or will touch. But you will know them in their fullness, as they will know you. Your words will draw many. My words through you will draw the multitudes.

James 5:16, Matthew 21:8–9, 1 John 3:2, and Matthew 10:20

# Wear Me Well

Soak Me in each day. Let Me fill you each morning so that My essence—My love, goodness, peace, patience, kindness, and self-control—overflows from you and covers those I put in your path. All people have a need for Me, but not all will seek Me. Show those who do not know Me and do not seek Me, who I am. Then, My child, they will desire Me, and I will pour Myself out on them until they are overflowing onto others. Do you see how My name, My love, and My character are proclaimed? It doesn't have to be shouted, just shown. I have commanded each one of you to go out and preach the gospel to the lost and dying. You can do this without saying a word. Wear Me well, little one.

Colossians 3:12–14 and Mark 16:15–16

# My Specialty

Pour out a blessing on those I send to you. Drink your fill of My Living Water so that you lack nothing when you give. Replenish your stores of My grace so you do not grow dry. Don't hold back, for I withhold nothing from you. All that I have for you is yours for the asking. My Word says, "You have not because you ask not." Therefore, ask! Broken vessels are My specialty. If My people are unaware of their brokenness and need of restoration, then I do not have the opportunity to repair. A false sense of wholeness is a barrier to true wholeness in Me. Therefore, pour yourself out on the broken vessels I send you, and watch as I renew their spirits within them.

2 Corinthians 9:8, James 4:2, Psalm 31:12, and Isaiah 57:15

# Lord of the Harvest

We have work to do, and I require many laborers. Few have come forth. There are many fields that go unplowed for lack of workers. Go out into the fields. Be My laborer. Bring in the harvest, for I am Lord of the harvest! You are called to labor for others. Be a witness to them. Mark out My territory with your prayers. Be on guard, for the enemy watches closely for an opportunity to strike. He hunts diligently, stealthily. But do not be afraid, for I am with you. You are Mine, and he will not touch you. Look only to Me for sustenance. I will always provide, for I love you.

Luke 10:2–3 1, Chronicles 4:10, and 2 Kings 6:15–17

*My Will*

# Cross Purposes

Come closer to Me, child. Bear up under the weight of My hand. Let it guide you into the peace you seek. My will for you is to have more of Me. Cross purposes confuse you. Look closely at your purpose—what you desire—and see where it crosses with Mine. Call out to Me for clarity and wisdom. Bend your will to Mine. This is the only avenue to peace and freedom. Take hold of your thoughts as never before and refuse to allow the devil access. He has gained ground as you have been buffeted about. Do not grow weary. The battle is won, and I am the victor. Be victorious in the Lord Jesus! Celebrate not My birth, but My death and resurrection, for therein lies the victory. Sing hallelujah to the King, for I reign!

Psalm 32:4–5, Psalm 143:10, and 2 Corinthians 10:5

# Disobedience Impedes Progress

isobedience stands in the way of progress. You attain knowledge of My will for you through obedience to My Word. Turn your ear to My voice so you can hear My direction. Many voices surround you, but Mine will penetrate to your core. Do not let self-indulgence keep you from following Me. My Spirit moves within you, preparing you for My words and My will. Adhere to My direction. Time is of the essence as we enter into this phase of your life. My plans are many. Bear up under your burdens. They have a purpose. When we are aligned, your burdens are light. When we are not, they feel heavy; and you become weighed down.

Luke 11:28, 1 John 2:16, and Matthew 11:28–30

# Focus on Today

Focus on what I have put before you. Look at your priorities—block out the unnecessary and leave out what is unimportant. Let those things go and present yourself to me. Do not fail to recognize My will for you in this. Open yourself up to My Spirit. Hear Me as I speak My heart and mind to you. Do not be afraid of tomorrow. Tomorrow is Mine, and all that it holds has already been ordained by Me. Seek only to know My will for today, for you cannot operate in your tomorrows. Today is your day, a gift from Me. Behold My glory today. Anticipate tomorrow, but do not dwell there. You lose sight of what I have given you in today when tomorrow is your focus.

Ephesians 5:15–17, Romans 8:5, and Matthew 6:33–34

# The Pressure of My Hand

Call out to Me, the Lord who saves. I own the world and all that's in it. My hand covers all. It can be a covering or a hiding place. It can be a source of pressure as I convict you or of leading as I guide you. My hand is My will for you. At times you need different things from Me. I give you what You need, according to My will. If you stray, pressure is applied. Each person feels my pressure in a way that is unique to him. Obedience relieves the pressure. When my children are walking in My will for them, I am their cover, their hiding place. Call out to Me!

Psalm 24:1, 1 Chronicles 29:12, and 2 Thessalonians 3:3

# A Perfect Way

Where there is a will, there is a way. When it is My perfect will, it is a perfect way. Pursue Me for My purposes and not your own. It is only then that you will achieve what I have ordained for you to do. Make the most of your days by abiding in Me, for it is in abiding that you find your purpose and your peace. Lean not on your own understanding, because there is confusion in that; lean into Me for clarity and vision. Rest your hopes on Me. Let Me show you who I am and what can be accomplished when we are joined together.

Matthew 6:10, John 15:4, and Colossians 1:9–11

# Make a Covenant

Follow Me, My child. Your course has been set. Just walk it out. Make a pact with Me—a covenant that will bind you to Me—and I will empty you of what you don't need and fill you with what you do. Remove any obstruction that prevents you from performing My will. Give Me your heart, for I will never break it. Measure My love. Try and find enough vessels to contain it. You will find it immeasurable, for it is never ending and overflowing. Forsake all for Me and hold fast to My truths. Mark it down that this day your requests have been heard by your Father. Wait upon Me, and bear witness this day that My children will be set free.

Hebrews 6:17, Proverbs 23:26, and Isaiah 64:4

# Choose Well

Call on Me, My child. It is useless to worry. Produce fruit for Me. That is all I ask of you. Continue to walk as I have instructed you. We are nearer than before. The time is coming for all people to choose whom they will follow. Choose well, My child. Do not be afraid. There will be a day that I will make known My will for you. Be prepared to walk in it. You will have everything you need because My Spirit will sustain you.

Luke 12:25, 2 Corinthians 6:2, and Psalm 54:4

Holy Spirit

# Choose to Satisfy the Spirit

Examine what is available to you during the course of your day. There are innumerable choices to be made—from what you choose to watch, read, listen to, or consume to your manner of speech. Also, consider where you go and what you do. Cross off your list anything that does not bring Me glory. Look at what is before you as a buffet and choose only that which will satisfy My Spirit within you. As on a buffet, there are things that appear to be good, but when eaten lack flavor and leave you unsatisfied. Do not be fooled by what the world offers as appealing or desirable, but partake of that which will satisfy the Spirit.

1 Corinthians 6:12–13, Romans 8:5, and Galatians 5:19–23

# All Who Are Thirsty

**W**orthy is the Lamb! All you who are thirsty come drink at the well of the Lord! My streams run swiftly and are free flowing. Grace, peace, and mercy are on all those who dip their cups in My stream! I cannot nor would I stop the flow of Living Water. Satisfy your thirst at My fountain. My Spirit seeks a home in you. I search always for those willing to invite Me in. Do not deny My Spirit a place to rest, for I will deny you nothing asked in My name. Jesus, King of Kings and Lord of Lords, is My name! Behold the One who lives and reigns forever!

Revelation 5:12, Jeremiah 17:7–8, Ephesians 3:16–17, and I Timothy 6:15–16

# Flow with the Spirit

My Spirit resides within you. As I move and breathe in you, move and breathe with Me. This is not a complicated journey, but it does demand focus. Awkward movements are not of My Spirit. My Spirit flows like water, and the flow is uninterrupted and unfazed by obstacles. So should you be! Depend on Me to guide you.

Romans 5:5 and 2 Corinthians 3:17

# Ask for My Spirit

Cast off all doubt, for your hope is in Me. I will always answer your call. Your iniquity bears witness to the sins of man. Your salvation bears witness to the power of the Risen Lord. With grace and mercy I have saved you. Yes, I snatched you from the hands of our enemy before he could devour you. Rejoice in Me! Bend your knees in worship and repentance. Seek Me for restoration and renewal. My spring is the fountain of life. Drink from it continuously. You do not have to wait or search for it; ask and you shall receive. I do not withhold My Spirit from anyone who calls out for Me. I will pour out My Spirit on you. Choose to be Mine, and you will receive it.

Psalm 51:5, Jonah 2:9, and Psalm 36:8–9

# I Am Worthy

C all on Me when you are weary; I will give you strength. Make known to Me your desires and needs; let Me fill them. We are on a journey. Walk with Me and let Me be your God. My glory is inherent in My Word. Read it, soak it up  and let it seep into your bones until it becomes a part of your very being. Hold it in high esteem. My Word will bring life and renew your spirit. Your spirit lags for lack of Me. Let Me refresh you by My Spirit, and I will fill you with all manner of joy and sustenance. Do not deny Me this pleasure, for I am your God who loves you and longs to give to you Myself. Hold tightly to Me. Cling to your Heavenly Father, for with Me is joy and safety, knowledge and goodness. My power dwells in My Spirit. Acknowledge Me. Desire Me for yourself, for I am worthy.

Psalm 18:3, Colossians 3:16, Romans 15:13, and Acts 1:8

# Move Softly

Make a way in the desert. My people are like the desert, dry and parched and in need of Living Water. Cordon off your time with Me. Protect it, for you need it. Set your mind on things above. Move softly through your day. Flow with My Spirit, not your mind. Question, but by prayer and supplication find your answers. Look at all things with My eyes, so you will know the truth of them. Beware of using your own understanding as you view situations, for My Spirit alone will guide you into all truth.

Isaiah 58:11, Colossians 3:2, and John 16:13

# Redeem, Refresh, Restore

Measures of time have been given to you; use them wisely. I gave them freely but with a purpose. I desire that you be purposeful in them. Remove all doubt and fear from your mind, for that is the enemy's tactic. The Spirit I have given you is one of boldness, love, and a sound mind. My Spirit instructs you. Heed Me. Become sensitive to My leading and pour yourself out. You will never be empty if you continue to seek your fulfillment through Me. Seek joy in your Lord, and experience the fullness of My presence. Redeem, refresh, restore—that is My plan for all of My people. But until I am permitted to move, they will not experience what I have for them: the redemptive, restorative, refreshing power of My Spirit. Pray for My people.

Psalm 90:12, John 14:26, and Colossians 1:13–14

# Peel Off the Mourning Clothes

Hold closely to the truths you have been given along the way. They will stand you in good stead. Pour forth the water you have received at My well on My people. It is pure and brings a freshening of the Spirit. Wash yourself clean with its purifying power. Minimize or get rid of anything that is in your way and keeps you from freedom. Peel off the mourning clothes, put on your garments of praise, and worship Me. Lift your banner high and praise Me. Adorn yourself with love, peace, and thanksgiving. Bow down before Me, and I will lift your head in joy.

John 4:14, Matthew 5:4, and Psalm 30:11–12

# See with Your Spirit

old fast to My truths. Do not neglect the reading of My Word. Take hold of the divine nature that has been in you since you welcomed Me as your Lord and Savior. Be bold in your speech. Fill it with love and truth. Admonish others with grace and gentleness, but stand strong with My Word as your foundation. Plant your feet; do not be swayed by emotion or what can be seen with your eyes. See with your spirit. Allow My Spirit to lead you: I will unfold a vision and equip you with "eyes to see."

Joshua 1:8, 2 Peter 1:3–4, and Joel 2:28–29

# The Key

Have faith in Me. Hear Me and believe Me. Do not question Me, but seek Me in all things. I will draw you where I want you; stay secure in that knowledge. My Spirit will speak to you. There is a time and a place for all things to be revealed. You will know and understand when it is the proper time. When you pray in the Spirit, the enemy's power is broken. That is the key. My Spirit moves quickly when you speak My language. Hold on to that truth; it will serve you well. Use it to break the yoke of sin and shame that binds My people.

James 1:6, Acts 2:4, and Romans 8:26–27

# The Saving Grace

eed My voice. You will need to stay alert to My whispers, for I do not call loudly. Grow sensitive to My Spirit. Give Me free rein in you. Prepare your mind to receive instruction, for it will come. I stand ready to complete My work; it will be done shortly. Do not be afraid but be forewarned. Prepare yourself for the inevitable. Keep yourself alert and aware; be on guard, for the enemy waits to attack. He will press home his point, but you will not be touched by the tip of his spear. It is by your faithfulness to Me that you will be saved. My blood has always been the saving grace. He cannot penetrate the purity and holiness of My blood. It has always been his downfall.

Galatians 5:25, Psalm 91:14, and Revelation 12:11

# The Spirit Leads Gently

My Spirit leads gently, not by force. You cannot force anyone to come to Me, but you can show them Me in ways that are far more effective. My Spirit resides within you. The visible manifestations of My Spirit that draw people to Me are gentleness, love, patience, long suffering, kindness, joy, peacefulness, goodness, and self-control. You cannot push a person from behind. Your fear pushes, but My Spirit draws forward. Show them the fruit of My Spirit. Pour it out on them—then they will want more of Me.

Proverbs 11:25 and Galatians 5:22–23

# Rivulets

Water flows downstream from its source. The small beginnings, the rivulets, become streams. The streams merge and form rivers, which combine and become oceans. My Living Water flows from My Spirit into you and through you onto others, then through them onto yet others, in an ever-widening and deepening ocean of believers. Each person who receives My Spirit and is refreshed by Me in turn gives Me access to others whom I have put in each one's path. Rejoice in this!

Isaiah 44:3 and Isaiah 41:17–18

# True Happiness

Make a way for me in the desert. This dry and parched land has need of a Savior. People believe they need "things" to be happy, but happiness is not found in the things you accumulate or in your ability to accumulate them. True happiness is found within. Whatever is inside you will determine your definition of happiness. If you are filled with My Spirit, then your spirit man has a direct connection to Me and all that I have for you. If you do not have My Spirit within you, there is emptiness, a void that your flesh keeps trying to fill. What satisfies the flesh? More of what the world has to offer. What satisfies the spirit? More of what I have to offer.

Psalm 63:1, Luke 12:15, Galatians 5:16, and 1 John 2:16–17

# You Have Need of Humility

You are blessed, My child, but you have need of humility. Therefore, I supply that need by allowing circumstances to challenge your perception of who you are. Continually check yourself for your motives and purposes. My Spirit guides you in this. Therefore, your answers are My truth in you. Take heart, My little one. Laughter and joy are yours; they are My gift to you. Your future is secure in Me. Reach out to Me, for I am ever near. Call on Me and see if I don't answer. I cannot resist the call of My people. I am ever ready to make new the old, to restore and refresh.

Proverbs 15:33, Ephesians 5:13, and 2 Corinthians 5:17–19

*Love*

# God's Love

Speak of your love for Me. Measure that out. It seems big and full, but there is an end to it. It waxes and wanes. It intensifies and weakens. It grows, and it can die. The human capacity to love is innate but imperfect. But My love never changes. It is complete and whole, and you can depend on it.

Revelation 2:4 and Ephesians 3:16—19

# Love Others

Care about those I put before you. Make an effort to see them as I see them. Love them as I love them: without judgment—accepting them as they are. Fault finding is a trap; whether it is applied to you or to someone else, it is a waste of time. Devote yourself to edifying everyone. Negativity has no place, so give it no room. Invite My Spirit into all communication. Do not speak words that have not been vetted by Me. Hold your tongue lest it open doors that you are not ready for.

John 13:34–35, Proverbs 11:12–13, and Proverbs 13:3

# An Illusion

easure yourself by My standards. Do not let others speak into your life words that do not come from Me. Hold yourself separate from the world and its views. Free yourself from the ties that bind. What seems to be tightly knotted is only an illusion: your sins, your memories, and the people who dwell in them are all used by Satan to keep you in bondage. Let the ropes drop and walk forward to Me. Anger, fear, doubt, and disbelief are what those ropes are made of. Shed the burden you carry when you hold on to these destructive emotions and mind-sets. Search Me out. Learn about Me. Come close and get to know who I am! My character is conveyed through My actions. Your doubt and disbelief are rooted in the lies of the enemy. As you come to know Me and My truth, you will be better able to discern his lies. My arms are wide open to you. Come, rest in My embrace. Feel the warmth of My love and the strength of My protection. You are safe with Me, and I want you to lay your head on My chest and hear My heart beat with love for you. Take heart, My child! I am with you always.

Romans 8:1, Romans 12:2, Psalm 103:12,
and Jeremiah 9:24

# Broadcast Love

Speak softly to those around you. Question your purpose before you speak. When you are aligned with Me and your purpose reflects Mine, then speak. Then and only then are My thoughts and words yours also. Measures of faith have been given to you. Ask for more. There is more to give. Fear has no stronghold where faith is. My love has captured you. You are restrained by it and simultaneously set free because of it. Rejoice! I love you, My child. Go forth and broadcast My love; spread it far like seeds planted by a farmer. Tend them, water and fertilize them, and prepare for a harvest. As you sow your seeds of love, you will bear good fruit. Mention My name so all will know your source.

Proverbs 17:27–28, Psalm 56:3–4, and Psalm 119:45

# Freedom

Freedom comes when you let go of your expectations. Your expectations for yourself, others, and situations keep you bound. If you can begin to let go of what you think will happen or what you want to happen, then you will find peace and the ability to move, adapt, and adjust more easily. When you remove preconceived beliefs, ideas, and expectations, then I am able to move more freely in you. You desire other people's acceptance and inclusion and expect to be fulfilled by that. When you don't feel accepted and included, rejection and hurt feelings follow. These emotions open the door for resentment and jealousy. When you allow My love for you and My inclusion of you in My family to fill you, then there is no room or need for the acceptance of others.

Ephesians 4:31–32, Hebrews 12:15, and Ephesians 1:4–6

# Your True Identity

*I* love you, My child. Perfect peace occurs in My arms. Let Me enfold you and encompass you in My loving embrace. Feel My love as it fills you and warms you. Nothing can ever separate you from My love because it is permanent and everlasting. Nothing—not your choices, your behavior, or even your sins—can change or affect My love for you. Rejoice in the truth that who I am defines who you are. Your beliefs, thoughts, and behaviors have evolved from your experiences. Others' words have tried to define you, but it is My Word that speaks truth about who you are: a chosen people, a royal priesthood, a holy nation, My special possession! Read My Word to learn your true identity and share My Word with others. Their need for Me is profound.

Romans 8:38–39, Colossians 1:22, and 1 Peter 2:9

# Love Washes Over You

reakthroughs are coming. Do not doubt My plan for you. My love washes over you with a cleansing flow that fills you up as you are emptied of your sinful nature. Learn the difference between what I have for you and what the world says you need. One brings the peace and contentment you seek. The other takes you back to the emptiness that keeps you seeking. Choose, My precious child. Choose with open eyes and an open heart. Expressions of My love abound; they are all around you. Ask Me to reveal them to you. Do not doubt My love for you.

Psalm 51:10, Psalm 16:11, and 1 John 4:9–10

# I Kept My Eye on You

Peer into the window of My heart and see how it beats only with love for you. You are Mine, an everlasting treasure, rescued and redeemed from the hands of the enemy. Tortured by his lies, imprisoned by your sins, you were lost. But I never lost sight of you. I kept My eye on you constantly, and at the right moment, I snatched you away and out of the power of his darkness. Now you can see the truth. My truth is not foreign to you. Deception no longer reigns over your life. It has no power, no shame, no foothold. You are free, My child. Walk in the freedom I gave to you by My death and the shedding of My blood. It was all for you. You no longer have to seek attention elsewhere, for you have Mine. Rejoice!

Deuteronomy 7:6, Psalm 33:13–14, and Romans 8:1–4

# John 3:16

To glean what I have for you from My Word, start with John 3:16. I gave My Son for you. Eat that truth, digest it, and let it become a part of you. Acknowledge Him in all your ways so that all you do reflects His nature. His willingness to sacrifice Himself for your salvation sets an example and an expectation. How willing are you to sacrifice for Him? What are you willing to give up to have Him, to learn His ways, and to honor Him? Contemplate this as you have at no other time. You live or die by your actions. Spiritually, each decision you make either leads toward life or death. Continue to choose the things of life, for in them you will find your true pleasure.

1 John 2:15–16 and Deuteronomy 30:19

# Love Immeasurable

My love for you is immeasurable. Give Me your heart, for I will never break it. You are My sweet, sweet child. Melt into My arms, for it is there you will find what you are looking for: pure love and complete acceptance. Look only into My eyes, for it is there you will see your true reflection. Do not look to others for what only I can give you. They are not focused on you as I am. Release your agenda and receive Mine. Forsake all for Me. Do not let the enemy fool you into thinking that you are pursuing My will when it is his. My will for you will never contradict My Word.

1 John 3:16, Ephesians 1:3–6, and Genesis 4:7

# Love Will Fill You Up

I love you with a love you cannot fathom. I want you to let My love flow through you to all you meet. I will fill you up so that joy and gladness will overflow out of you. I will wipe away all the tears you have cried in sorrow, for My love will cover it all. I am more than enough for You. Continue to walk with Me, and in worship bow down before Me. Acknowledge Me in all you do and know that I am in charge. We are on a journey that extends into eternity. We will walk together forever. You will be My child, and I will be your God and Father. Heaven is your home.

1 John 4:9–11, Luke 6:21, and Proverbs 3:6

# Receive My Love

My holiness will be evident to all who can see. Open your eyes, My child, and gaze upon your Creator, who loves you more than you can ever know or understand. There is no human way to measure My love. It is present at all times and worthy of being praised. My love needs to be received to be felt. Receive it as it is given—freely and in great quantities, more than you can hold. It tumbles out and overflows onto all who believe in Me. Search for Me, seek Me, and I will be found by you. Evidence of My love will abound as you go forth. There will be no doubt of My presence as you fulfill My purpose. Speak of My love to My people. They thirst for a love like Mine, and so they seek it in others. They look for it in the world around them. They need to know that what they seek can only be found in Me.

Ephesians 3:17–19, 1 John 4:7–8, and Psalm 53:1

# Comfort

The comfort you seek is with Me. I am ever present. My Spirit resides in you, and brings the comfort of My love. Feel My presence within, for I am there with you. My love will provide what you need, but do not keep it just for you: extend it to others. Also, speak gentle words to yourself. Do not berate yourself for mistakes. I do not. My gifts to you overcome your flaws and weaknesses. Be determined to move forward with Me as we continue this journey. Do not lag behind or allow life to distract you. I am waiting for you. You have obstacles to overcome within yourself that need to be addressed. Be faithful in this, and you will succeed in overcoming the enemy. Do not be afraid to move forward now. There will be more challenges ahead. That is My design for you. You must learn to trust Me in all circumstances. Revelation is necessary for redemption. They go hand in hand.

2 Corinthians 1:3–4, 1 John 5:4, and Proverbs 29:18

# Choose to Love

hoose to love, regardless of circumstances. Love is a conscious decision. If you have Me in you, then your ability to love others is there. You, My child, then must choose to dip into that well and pour out the love on those I put in your path. Do not grow weary of doing good, for it is in the doing of it that you are rewarded. Give of yourself to others, so that you begin to exercise the muscle of selflessness. You will make it strong and develop muscle memory. Eventually, the giving of your self will be automatic. Look for ways to give without examining inconvenience. Your comfort zone is still too small. Let us expand your territory.

1 Corinthians 13:4–7, Ephesians 5:1–2, and Philippians 2:3–4

Mercy

# Freedom in Forgiveness

Forgiveness and forbearance are for those who have hurt you. Do not rely on them to release you with apologies, but allow Me to free you from that burden. For it is only within Me that you secure your freedom from all that holds you back from My plan for you. Your hopes and dreams are within Me, not in people.

Ephesians 4:32, Mark 11:25, and Isaiah 61:1

# Conviction versus Condemnation

Don't measure the weight of your sin according to man's opinion, but measure it against My love for you. There is no comparison between how others view you and My view of you. Let Me speak to you of your sins, because My love can cover the greatest sin. My voice carries truth born of love, purposed to convict and not to condemn. Conviction leads you back to Me; condemnation leads you away from Me. Never forget that I see you through My Son. His purity and light illuminate all the dark places. You see much more clearly because of Him. As Jesus reveals your iniquity and My Spirit convicts you, My love and forgiveness are poured out upon you. Thus, there is no room for condemnation. Guilt has no place; shame, no foothold.

1 John 1:9, Psalm 32:1–2, and John 8:11–12

# Repent

Who among you has sinned? All have. Repent and re-ceive My forgiveness. Call out for My mercy, and you will be forgiven. Narrow your focus to look at the freedom I have put before you. Engage your senses to fully receive what I have for you: My blessing of forgiveness. All My blessings are upon you. Do you not detect a shift? For it has been made known to you this day that I am the Lord God, Creator of the universe, all-powerful, all-knowing, and perfect in every way. I am merciful, and I am love in its purest form. Rejoice and be glad. Therefore, I will have My way. Remain in Me, and I will remain in you.

Romans 3:23, Isaiah 45:18, and 1 John 4:16

# Position Yourself

osition yourself to be humble. Humility is not natural because it requires putting others before you. Thinking only of yourself produces distorted thinking and pride. I am your Maker. I know your thoughts before you think them. I know your feelings before you experience them. And I know how you will respond before a situation occurs. So why wouldn't you come to Me? My ways may disturb you because they sometimes cause discomfort or pain. But if you obey and follow My ways, you will see that the pain and discomfort are temporary. If you continue to follow your own path, you will endure pain and discomfort always. Forgiveness comes with repentance. True repentance requires humility.

2 Chronicles 7:14, 1 Chronicles 28:9, and 2 Corinthians 7:9

# Forgiveness

Forgiveness is not predicated on confessing your sins to man or going to a church. Forgiveness is predicated on going to your knees in repentance before your loving and just Father, who will look into your heart and forgive you because He loves you to a depth that you cannot fathom and struggle to believe.

Psalm 103:8–12

Obedience

# Blessings Are Contained in Obedience

My desire is to be one with you so that you have no fear or hesitation to do what I ask of you. Your blessings are contained in your obedience to Me and are not arbitrary or contrary to My nature. Your heart is open before Me. I see it all in My light. I am uncovering any hidden or dark places so that you will be aware of them. This is uncomfortable but necessary. Our work requires you to have knowledge of your weaknesses and sins. When you are aware, you know to press into Me and make the effort necessary to overcome the weakness or eliminate the sin. It is your obedience to Me and willingness to let Me have My way with you that allows us to move forward. You will draw closer to Me through all of this. That is My heart's desire.

John 17:21, Deuteronomy 11:26–27, and Ephesians 5:13–14

# Financial Stewardship

Pay what is owed. Do not spend what I provide for that reason. I am with you always to lead and guide you. Be faithful. Come to Me for all your needs, and I will be faithful to answer. Be discerning with your money. You have a desire for more, but is that not the way of the world? Do not be like the world; be satisfied with what you have. I will provide. Trust Me in this. Listen for Me, My child. My instructions through My Spirit bring life, joy, and peace. A life lived with Me is fulfilling and real. Without Me, it is an illusion. My wisdom can be yours if you ask. I have all the answers, including those about your financial needs. Listen carefully and act on what I say. Do not simply hear it, but act. It is in walking out My instructions that you have victory in Me, for it is already done, except for your obedience.

Romans 13:8, James 1:22, and Deuteronomy 5:33

# Movement Requires Obedience

Obedience is an option, not a requirement; although movement requires obedience. Therefore, if you choose not to obey, you stay where you are. It is your choice, and I love you either way. But My plan requires obedience. Where are you, My child? What I ask of you is not heavy or burdensome, but it does require action on your part. What keeps you from moving forward? Are you resting? You cannot do what I ask of you from a sitting position. Are you waiting? Waiting for what? Trust Me. It is My plan for you. My promises are contained in My plan. You must obey to receive My promises. Remember Me from of old. I have not changed, nor have My instructions or My plan. Choose to obey. That is My will for you.

Luke 11:28, Psalm 19:7–11, and Psalm 33:11

# The Way Out

Decide who you will follow, My child. You cannot pick and choose in the moment; you must be consistent. Come back to your first love. I remain the same. I am who I say I am. Surrender all to Me. Your mind, body, will, and emotions need to be Mine. Let My Spirit move in you to wash away your iniquity and pain. Allow Me free access to all of you. Rejoice in My ability to free you from sin and the ties that bind you to the darkness. Let Me have My way in you. Obedience is a skill learned in the depths of your trials. You stay in the depths until you realize that the way out is through obedience to Me. Only I know the truth. Live by My rules, not the world's. They are made by man and fashioned for his purposes. My rules are divine in origin and are fashioned after My Spirit, My character, and My nature.

Joshua 24:15, Revelation 2:4–5,
1 Corinthians 6:11, and 1 Peter 1:14

# Peace Comes through Obedience

Contemplate what I have put before you. Reach out for what is in front of you. There are many who never receive all that I have for them because they do not respond to My instructions. My love for them does not lessen, but their joy and blessings are diminished. Your joy is obtained through My peace. My peace comes through obedience. You act in obedience when you love and trust Me. Catch hold of all that I have for you. Stay alert and aware so you are always listening and hearing what I am saying. Move forward in your work and be content where you are.

John 14:23, Luke 11:28, and Philippians 4:11

# Spirit of Diligence

ake wise choices, and I will bless you and extend your time so that all may be accomplished. My work is easy, but you need to be diligent to accomplish it. Pray for a spirit of diligence, and I will anoint you to move through your days with grace and peace to accomplish all that I give you and all that you have to do. You will have plenty of time for rest and refreshment at the end of your day. Hear and obey Me in this, and your reward will be great in Heaven. My hand is on you to lead and guide. Take heart and move forward with Me, and I will show you My goodness. Your time is not your own—it is Mine. Give it to Me, and you will witness My power and glory as I use your time for My purposes! Pray on this.

Hebrews 6:11–12 and Matthew 25:21

# Storms Happen

Storms happen, but My hand rests on those I love, to shield and protect them from the fury of the storm. Minute by minute I watch over My children to guide and direct each path. It is only by divine protection that you escape the fate of many. Obedience can prevent some of the storms of life, so do not linger in disobedience. The consequences are long-term, though they are not evident at first. Make decisions that put you firmly in My will for you. There are moments of joy and pain in everyone's life. Not one will be wasted if I am allowed to direct your path. My infinite goodness and mercy cover all sins.

Psalm 91 and Genesis 50:20

# Consequences

The devil's plan is to destroy you and your family in subtle ways, as he has done since the beginning. Guard against him by your walk with Me. Settle the matter of obedience, because it lingers and causes delay. Your heart and mind need conviction. Bow before Me in all things, not just some or most. Do what I ask of you, for My plans are good. I will always forgive you and never stop loving you, but I will choose not to use you if you are disobedient. This is your choice. Do not stray from what I have instructed you to do. You know the truth of My words. You have seen My hand at work, you have heard My voice, and you know Me. I am God, the Everlasting Father, the Prince of Peace, your soon and coming King! I am worthy of your diligence. Hold fast to Me. Be excellent because I am excellent. My Spirit is in you!

Genesis 3:1, James 1:22–24, and Isaiah 9:6

# Obedience and Diligence Are the Keys

Hold on to Me. I am indeed your answer. Persevere in your effort to change in those areas of your life that are not aligned with My will for you, for I am with you in this. Your effort and My grace are sufficient for the journey. Continue to push forward and do not give up. Your goal is attainable in Me, for it is My goal for you. Do not faint or grow weary in pursuing My purposes. I do not hold a carrot in front of you; I hold eternity before you. Pledge your allegiance to Me, the God of eternity! Do not fall prey to self-indulgence and excuses, but persist with obedience and diligence. My Spirit convicts you to keep you aware and moving in the right direction.

2 Peter 1:10–11, James 1:14, and John 16:8

*Pain*

# I Exist in All Circumstances

Try to measure out what I have given you. You will find it is immeasurable. Count out your treasures. You cannot, because there is no end to what I have for you. Mark a place in your history where I have not been. You cannot, for I have always been where you are. You have not existed without My knowledge or My approval. Even though you experience pain and suffering, I do not stand idly by and watch My children suffer. No! My work in them and in their circumstances occurs even if it isn't seen. I am misunderstood by those who suffer. My way is not to deliver them out of their circumstances, but to deliver within them. Death, destruction, pain, and suffering will come in this world, but their presence does not negate My presence or My goodness. I exist in all circumstances. I reign regardless of the conditions. You live in a fallen world whose people are under the influence of one whose goal is to destroy. His ways deceive and blind people to their realities. My ways reveal and alert My people to their realities. His ways are lies and destruction. My ways are truth and life. Your hope is in Me. Rejoice in that truth.

Psalm 31:19–20, 1 Peter 1:6–7, and 2 Corinthians 4:4

# Purpose in Allowing Pain

Ears have not heard nor have hearts received what I have for My people. Never before has there been a time such as this. Fear has no place here, only joy at the coming of the Lord Jesus Christ! The weapons used against you will not prosper. Your pleading does not go unnoticed, and your prayers will not go unanswered. My children must learn to walk with Me; therefore, make no move to prevent the work of My hand. I always allow My people to make choices in life, although I know some of those choices will bring pain. In their pain, some will turn to Me and begin to seek Me in repentance, for forgiveness and reassurance. Pain is not My purpose—salvation and healing is.

1 Corinthians 2:9, Isaiah 54:17, 1 John 5:14–15, and
2 Corinthians 7:9–10

# Moments of Rest

*I* provide moments of respite for those in pain, for I will not hold back as I begin My work in each of My children. Respite comes when each level is achieved and before the next level is encountered. Most people believe they are finished as each trial is over. But there is only a time of rest between levels, for one cannot rise to the next level without the trial preceding it. My children cannot go from glory to glory without encountering obstacles and rocks on the path. Perseverance is necessary to achieve the ends I have established. Therefore, call out to those on the path. Encourage, edify, and remind them who they are and whose they are. It is written that all who call on the Lord will be heard. Call out, and I will answer!

James 1:12, Romans 5:3–5, and Psalm 145:18–19

# Pain Is Needed for Growth

Pain is necessary for growth, as one must often feel pain to be made aware of a problem. As in your body, pain indicates a problem. So it is in your heart as well. It isn't until you feel the hurt that you become aware of something that needs to be addressed. Discomfort and heartache are ways of getting your attention. Isn't that true for you? People move along in life with little thought of Me until their lives become painful or uncomfortable. You are learning that if you turn to Me first in all things, and walk according to My will, you will experience less pain and heartache. Rejoice in this and live by that rule.

I Peter 1:6 and Deuteronomy 28:1–2

# Provision

# Each Is Equipped for the Journey

Rest in Me, for your path is set—captured by grace, sustained with love, and ordained by My hand. Take note of where you are in your journey. There are twists and turns, but I have never lost sight of you. You are equal to the task. Never doubt who you are or what you are capable of. Many form the family of God. Each has a mission to fulfill My purpose for the Body of Christ. As I call, I provide. Each person is equipped for the journey. Not all provision is revealed. But as obstacles and challenges are met on the path, My hand plants the seed to bring forth whatever is needed to overcome them. Rejoice that I have placed in you exactly the right spiritual gifts and talents required to be an overcomer! The key is faith. Your faith in Me unlocks all doors and makes all that I have for you possible. Pray for more faith!

Hebrews 13:20–21, Romans 12:6–8, and Hebrews 11:6

# The Abundant Life

Spending time with Me is necessary for you to receive the abundant life I provide. It is my joy to fill you up each morning with all you need for the day. Do not give in to the schemes of the enemy. He finds joy in your pain and discomfort. I find joy in your trust and dependence on Me. You are My sweet child, and I love you. We are on a journey, and it has not ended. My people toil and struggle for their daily bread, not knowing that I will provide out of My abundance if they will but trust in Me.

John 10:10, Psalm 62:5–6, and John 6:32

# Provision Is Spiritual

My provision is more about who I am than what I provide. Human thinking has narrowed this concept to mean only money or material possessions. But the true definition of My provision is spiritual in nature. By My death on the cross and resurrection, I provided My Holy Spirit to you. By His presence in your life, you are provided spiritual gifts and the fruit of the Spirit. Through the spiritual gifts and the fruit of My Spirit, you have the means and the way to know Me, My will for you, and My purpose through you, and to walk in the manner I ordained for you. Nothing is more important to you than to have the Holy Spirit in you. It is because of Him that you can know Me. Through Him, My power is in you. Without Him, you bear no fruit.

John 16:7, Galatians 5:22–23, 1 Corinthians 12:7, and Acts 1:8

# The Storehouse Is Full

Pour out your heart to Me. Measure it all out and compare it with what I have for you. The exchange rate will always be in your favor. You cannot lose. I will always give you more than you give Me. I will give you more faith to replace your fear. I will give you more love for the anger you give Me. I will give you more peace to replace your anxiety. I will also give you more humility to replace your pride; more courage to replace your doubt; more confidence to replace your insecurities; more truth to replace the lies.

I never run out of what you need. My storehouse is full. Never doubt My love or My plan for you. Each was in place before the world began. We continue to walk together; therefore, no step you take will be unknown to Me. No breath you breathe will be a surprise. I have complete knowledge of you, so never doubt Me or My covering.

Ephesians 3:20, Deuteronomy 28:12, Jeremiah 29:11, and
Psalm 33:13–15

# Wineskins

It is unwise to pour old wine into new wineskins, because the wine will burst the skins. Old wine is made up of old ideas, actions, and beliefs for a time that has passed and is no longer viable. I have put new wine in you for these new times. It must be poured out so its potency can be used. New wine is flavorful and goes down easy. The old wineskin was suited for the old wine. I have done a new thing in you and formed a new wineskin to hold the new wine. Each of you is a new wineskin, fashioned by the trials and challenges that you have experienced in recent times. You are no longer who you used to be. You no longer think or act in the same manner. It was imperative that you shed old ways and beliefs to embrace the new. Our journey continues. The path is the same. It was laid out before time began.

Luke 5:37–38, Romans 5:3–5, and Titus 3:3–5

# Relationship with God

# My Character

I do not give partial promises. My promises are full and complete in Christ. Do not waver or hesitate to grasp the reality of who I am. I am your Provider, and My promises are contained in Me. Receive Me, and receive all that I have for you. You are My child, My precious one whom I have called to Myself. There is no turning in Me: who I am, what I say, and My plans for you never change. Trust Me to be who I say I am. My Word contains all you need in order to know Me. I am in My Word; I am My Word. Your fears are based on lies. I cannot lie, so the enemy entered into your story before you were able to understand the difference between us. The enemy has had you for a time. Now it is My turn to teach you, reach you, love you, and heal you.

2 Corinthians 1:20, James 1:17, and Proverbs 30:5

# Get to Know Me

o not forsake your time with Me, because it is in those moments that My blessings are released. You have to know Me to have faith in Me and to want to obey Me. How can you get to know someone unless you spend time together? Spend time with Me and get to know who I am. Revere and worship Me. When our relationship is established, your faith will build from it. When we are in a relationship, you will then have the courage to obey Me, because you will know that I am who I say I am and that I do what I say I will do.

Matthew 6:6, Proverbs 8:17, and Exodus 20:20

# Intimate Relationship

I n an intimate relationship with Me, there is honest talk and open dialogue, a willingness to listen and hear My heart and instructions. You are not always willing to do that. At times your weaknesses and faults make you unwilling to hear the truth. Long-distance relationships do not require intimacy. Close daily contact demands it. Therefore, when you choose to separate yourself from Me by not meeting Me at the well each day, you are choosing a long-distance relationship. Draw close so that you receive all that you need from Me daily.

James 4:8, John 5:40, and John 15:4

# Passionate Pursuit

Passionate people gain credibility when they pursue their passion. What is yours? Make the most of your time with Me. Pursue Me with passion, and your reward will be great. Reap the reward found in a relationship with Me, your Lord and Giver of Life, the Author and Finisher of your faith. Make no mistake that I listen for your voice. I know the voice of each of My children. I know you intimately and desire that you come to know Me. My sheep know My voice. Get to know Me so that you will be able to distinguish between My voice and those of the devil and the world. This is an invitation to all. Not all will accept it, and My heart grieves for the lost. Turn to Me, My child. Hear Me. Do not doubt My existence or My intentions. I call out. Answer the call.

Deuteronomy 4:29, Psalm 66:19–20, John 10:14, and I
Timothy 2:4

# No Boundaries

Foster a relationship with Me that knows no boundaries. Meet all adversity with trust in Me. You come through the storm by My power and might. Look not at what is around you, but look at Me. Your world is in chaos, but Mine is not. Your world is in disarray, but Mine is in order. Your world marches to destruction, but in Mine there is victory! Hold fast to the truths that I teach. Each one is a lifeline. Measure all loss as gain, for when you are emptied of all worldly desires, there will be room for those things that will truly satisfy. Present yourself to Me as an empty vessel and let Me fill you with all I have for you. Position yourself to receive a blessing according to My perfect will for you.

1 Chronicles 16:11, Matthew 24:6–7, and Philippians 3:8

# Relationship Is the Key

My children yearn for My embrace but fail to receive it. Why? Because they do not know Me! They do not recognize Me in the goodness of their lives. My people do not know their Father! No one speaks of My goodness and mercy. They speak of My judgment and of My provision, but they do not speak of My goodness. I am good: it is in My goodness that they receive My love. They feel My embrace in those moments of sweetness despite their circumstances. Hope is lost when My goodness and mercy are not received. Relationship is the key. All is lost without a relationship with Me. I made you for relationship. You are built, constructed, and ordained for this purpose. I grieve for those who do not choose Me. I seek those who will. My heart is for you. My love abounds and is for all, but few receive it. I am good and merciful! There is plenty for everyone; My stores are full to overflowing. Receive the blessing that only comes from Me, your Father in Heaven. Speak of my goodness; help My children to experience Me in this way.

Romans 2:4, Psalm 86:5, and John 1:10–13

# The Faithful One

Carve out time for Me. Caution is necessary as we move forward. Do not step quickly; move forward with a keen awareness of your need for My guidance. My Spirit will lead you where I want you to go. Ask for what you need according to My will, and it shall be yours. Keep pressing into Me. Do not stop seeking My face, for your answers lie with Me. Take hold of My hand and trust Me to know the way. I am the Way, the Truth, and the Life. Redemption comes with obedience, and obedience comes after surrender. Surrender is possible where there is trust—you can trust Me because I am the Faithful One. Everything begins in Me! I am the Answer, your answer. Believe in Me and My power to do all that you ask and more, according to My Word.

John 16:13, 1 John 5:14, Psalm 86:15, and Ephesians 3:20–21

# Plant Your Feet

Press in, and in a little while, you will see the light and understand. It has not been hidden; you just haven't reached it yet. The way has been difficult, but not impossible. Plant your feet and stand your ground. Do not be moved by your circumstances but by My Spirit. I am confident in you; are you confident in Me? Do you think that I do not see you or that I am unaware of your circumstances? If that is still a question in your mind, then you have not fully come to know Me. Sit with Me as I teach you what you need to know. Bow before Me in reverence and surrender. Set your gaze on Me, for Mine is on you.

Ephesians 6:13, Psalm 32:8, and Psalm 5:7

# Walk with Me

Walk with Me, My child. I do not command you; I ask it of you. What do you have to lose? What do you have to gain? Measure the two. Where am I in that picture? If you keep your eyes on Me, as I have asked, then you will choose to obey, and we will walk together. Do not be satisfied with where you are now. Continue to grow and develop your relationship with Me. It can grow deeper and more abundant as you continue to seek Me for what you need and want. I am here for you, as always.

Hebrews 10:21–23, 2 Corinthians 4:18, and
2 Thessalonians 1:3

Seek God

# Come to the Well

Come to the well, My child. Refresh yourself at My feet and let Me feed you with the food that sustains. It is good and satisfies completely, strengthening you for what lies ahead. On your journey with Me, use caution as you move forward. Be certain of your footsteps before you take them. Look for the enemy before you proceed. He hides in corners you cannot see and under rocks that you may stumble on. Be positioned in such a way that he cannot escape detection: when your knee is bent in humility and your eyes are on Me, nothing will escape your notice.

Isaiah 55:2, 2 Corinthians 11:14–15, and Psalm 95:6–7

# Comfort in My Arms

low with My Spirit. Seek the comfort of My arms. You do well to cordon off your time: you will gain all you require for each day when you seek Me. There is much to do, but there is ample time in which to accomplish all that is before you. My rest is what you seek. My peace is what you search for. Both are obtained in the moments that you reserve for Me. Pour out your heart to Me, for My ears are always open to you. My heart is perpetually filled with love for you, and My hand is ever moving in your circumstances. You are My child, and I take care of My own. You will never be without My presence or My provision. That is a promise to all of My children.

Matthew 11:28, Psalm 62:8, and Psalm 121:3

# Find Fulfillment

*I* will pour all the blessings of Heaven onto My people, if they will but turn and recognize Me for who I am. Find shelter under My wings and satisfy yourself at My feet. Let Me feed you as only I can. Reach out and know I am here. Do not collapse under the weight of your burdens. Come to Me, and I will give you rest. What you are carrying will only get heavier without Me, so you must seek Me out. Search for Me, and you will find Me. When you find Me, you will find your answers and your heart's desire. Clear out your schedule and allow Me to fill your time with what I have for you. You will find fulfillment when you find your purpose in Me. There is no fulfillment for those who do not seek Me. They go hungry because what they eat is not of Me—it does not satisfy.

Ezekiel 34:26, Matthew 11:28–30, and John 6:27

# Imperfection

You are more than enough. Your mistakes create opportunities for growth. I move easily in one who is given over to Me. Perfection should not be a goal; My hand impedes those who seek it. Imperfect is how I created you. In My likeness, but not "like" Me. Rejoice in your imperfections. They bind you to Me—you seek Me because of them.

Proverbs 24:16, Genesis 5:1–2, and Philippians 3:12

# Let Me Lead

I will purify you with the fire of Heaven. My heavenly flames will not burn you, but they will burn away the chaff: that which is not needed and only hampers your progress. I am with you always, My child, as a father should be. Stay close to Me and seek Me in all things. Never fear the darkness, for My light will shine forth and illuminate it in and around you. You will always walk in the light, for My lamp never goes out. My Spirit seeks a home; provide one. Do not run off ahead of Me. That is fruitless, for your fear is leading you, not your faith. Trust Me in all things. Do not let others' opinions deter you or distract you. Go slowly and softly, but be steadfast in your faith. I am in this. You know Me; therefore, you must follow My rules. I will make your path straight when your heart is right. Examine your intentions in all you do. Do nothing automatically, but first come before Me and present your request. Bow down before Me, for I have your answers. Worship Me in spirit and in truth. I am worthy to be praised!

Matthew 3:12, Proverbs 4:26–27, Psalm 26:2,
and John 4:23–24

# Passive Faith

ountains that stand in your way crumble as you seek My face. Prepare your heart and mind to receive My Word. Hold on to Me. You tend to forget who I am: I am your King and your Provision. All you need to walk in a manner worthy of Me is Me! Seek Me early in My temple. Come and unburden yourself at the well. Drink till you are full before you start your journey each day. As you slip further away from Me, your doubts increase, you hesitate longer, and your mind is not as clear. Therefore, you stay stuck; you see a way but are not sure you should take it. Your inactivity renders your faith dormant. When you allow doubt and disbelief to enter into your thinking, the battle for your mind grows stronger. Being on guard, as I have instructed you, is not just about being alert and aware; it is also about being actively engaged with Me. Passive faith is a trap you have fallen into. Seek Me; worship Me; obey Me; talk to Me; bow before Me; trust Me. These activate your faith. All of these require you to engage with Me. Fight your tendency to withdraw into silence and become focused on your own thoughts and beliefs. That path has no destination. It is only when you engage with Me that you find direction and are able to stay on My path for you. Trust Me for your direction, for I promise to guide you.

Mark 11:23, Matthew 7:7–8, 2 Corinthians 10:5, and Psalm 9:10

# Performance Is Not Necessary

Performance is not necessary. It is not what I'm looking for, and it is not what I look at. It is your heart that I search. Seek Me out daily. Ask for My counsel always. Do not retreat inside of yourself, for there are no answers there, only a false sense of security and protection. I am your security and protection. Count on Me for those things you cannot do for yourself. Be enamored of Me, not of what you see Me do in others or for others. There is a trap there. Avoid it. Make no mistake that we walk together. Feel My arms around you, My sweet child. Remember, I am your Father who loves you infinitely more than you can ever imagine or understand.

1 Samuel 16:7, 2 Corinthians 3:4–5, and Ecclesiastes 4:4

# Pursue Me

o not fear the morning, for it brings a fresh anointing, a fresh wind of My Spirit. Do not fear the evening, for contained within the darkness is My presence. My voice can be heard in the stillness of your night season. Seek Me there, and you will find Me. Never forsake the pursuit. Keep seeking, for you will always find me. Listen for My voice, and you will hear My instructions. My Word never comes back void. My love for you is contained in My instructions: both are a part of the plan I have for you. I first loved you and brought you into this world, and I have set a plan in place for your life. My Spirit speaks your instructions to you. Make a place for Me and welcome Me. Be open to My leading. Forsake all others and listen only to My voice. My Spirit knows My heart and speaks it to you. I love you.

Psalm 91:5, Proverbs 8:17, 1 John 4:19, and Ephesians 1:11

# Renew Your Strength

e blessed, My child. I am here with you. You are never without My Spirit. Stay close to Me and listen carefully as I lay out My plan for you. Do not doubt Me or My wisdom, but take heed to move when I move. My pace quickens as we move closer to the day of revelation. All will be revealed in time, but you must wait on it. Waiting can cause weariness, and weariness causes impatience. Though you grow weary, you can renew your strength in Me, because I supply all your needs. The way may be blocked by those who do not believe, but I will make a way where there is no impediment. Trust Me in this. Watch Me move through the barriers with ease. Keep your focus on Me so I can impart My wisdom to you. Maintain a record of My voice so you do not forget. Call on Me in times of need. I will answer, for I am faithful in all that I do. Be alert and aware at all times. Heaven waits to help you. Seek Me, and you will find Me.

Psalm 139:7, Isaiah 40:31, and Psalm 91:15

# Safety My Arms

R est in Me. Seek Me in all things that matter to you; I will answer. My words are life giving! Know My voice and listen to it. Continue to step forward in your faith. You will not be disappointed. I hold the keys to your future; therefore, you are safe in My arms. Come closer, moving forward in your faith. Heed My call and do not hesitate. Listen carefully for My instructions. Leave your cares behind and press forward, for I am showing you the way. I will light your path as never before. You will grow in wisdom and discernment, and your heart will be filled with love and grace for all.

1 Chronicles 16:11, Psalm 31:14–15, and Isaiah 42:16

# Seek My Face

You will never run out of what you need because My supply is endless. You have now found your way to My will. The path is well worn. Do not stray off the path, for there is no other way to receive what you need each day. I wait for you daily with cup in hand to quench your thirst, to fill you, to provide your every need. Seek My face, child, not My hand. When you seek Me for Me, My hand automatically moves in your life. Seeking Me releases My promises. My promises are for all, but not all will receive.

Philippians 4:19 and Matthew 6:32–33

# I Have Your Answers

Trials and tribulations come to all. Forbearance is necessary. Be on guard that you do not mistake My hand for My judgment. As My hand moves, you experience trials and tribulation, but it is your response to My hand that determines the outcome. I am not judging you in this moment. I am moving in your life now so that you do not experience the consequences of your actions later. Therefore, respond in a manner that lifts My hand. Seek Me for your answers. My answers contain My wisdom and discernment. Know Me so that you recognize My answers. Confusion comes when you don't know Me: the love in My heart, the sound of My voice, or the content of My character. Come, My child! Walk through the open door of My heart so you can learn who I am! I long to show you My love in a manner in which you can receive it. For it is then that you will turn to Me and find Me.

Deuteronomy 4:30, Proverbs 2:6, and 1 Corinthians 14:33

# The Treasures of This World

Do not be blinded by this world and the treasures it holds, for they are appealing but empty. Yearn for My treasures that I have stored up for you in Heaven. They are everlasting and pure. Just because you can't see them doesn't mean they are not real. Trust Me in this. My love for you is endless: it will never fade or grow weak. It cannot because I am love itself, and My power is divine and never fades. Seek Me, your True Treasure, when you are in need. Seek Me when you are empty. Seek Me in times of trouble, for I am here. Seek Me when you are content and have no need. Seek Me when you are safe and secure, for I am here. Seek Me in all things and at all times, for I am ever near and watching over you. You are My precious one, My beloved. Call My name. I am here.

Matthew 6:20, Psalm 103:17, and Acts 17:27–28

# I Am Your Savior

ear Me, My child, for I am near to you. Listen to Me, for I speak words of wisdom to you. Open your ears and your heart, for these matters are important and lasting. Many will come to be fed. Feed My sheep; they are needy and in search of food. Salvation is at hand for those who seek Me. There is enough for all, but not all will come. They quench their thirst at another source. It is one that will go dry eventually. They do not realize that My Living Water never runs dry. Holy, Holy, Holy is My name in all the earth. Do not forsake Me, My child, I am your salvation! I am your Savior! Come to Me in all things. Trust Me in this. It is to your benefit that I speak, and My words are true. Speak to Me, and I will speak to you.

Colossians 2:2–3, John 7:37, and Romans 10:9

Surrender

# Yield

*I* am ever near for all you need. My comfort, provision, and faithfulness are always available to those who seek Me. Continue to seek Me, and you will always find Me as you walk steadily in My direction. Rest assured of My presence in your life. My hand is evident; therefore, yield under the pressure of it. Calmly allow yourself to be led by it. Resist the urge to avoid My pruning work that molds and refines you. My will is perfect for you. Abide in it, trust it, and surrender to it. Nothing I do is meant to harm you. All will become clear in time. Relax and find peace in Me, your Savior, Jesus Christ.

Psalm 145:17–19, Isaiah 64:8, and Jeremiah 29:11

# Freedom in Surrender

I want total allegiance from My children. I want all of who you are, including your mind. Go beneath the surface of your thoughts. Explore what's hidden there: find out what you're hiding and what you're hiding from. There is a key. Use it. You hold on to things of the past, such as torment from past mistakes, guilt, and regret that you haven't released to Me. These keep you in bondage. There is freedom in surrender; there is hope in release. Let Me break the bonds that tether you to your past. You are a new creation in Christ Jesus. Turn and look. See what I have created. You are My masterpiece.

Mark 12:30, 1 John 1:9, and Ephesians 2:10

# Have Faith in Me

When you bend your knee to Me, you are transformed from an independent, self-willed person to a dependent, surrendered child. Continue to seek Me in all things, My sweet one. It is the key to your success and your peace. You will not always do everything right, but I can make everything right when I am your answer. Turn to Me. Believe in Me. Have faith in Me. We are moving in the direction of eternity. Contemplate that with joy and gratitude. My words are important and hold great value for My people. Your life is in My hands; therefore, My peace is yours when you release all to Me. I am your God, your Father in Heaven who loves you with an infinite love—yes, an eternal love.

Psalm 95:6–7, Romans 8:28–29, and Psalm 19:7

# Release All

You have long held the belief that your voice is like one crying in the desert, and you have thought that no one has heard you. But I have listened intently for many years. I have kept you in My hand for the proper time, and I have not allowed any harm to come to you. My protection has been complete because My plan for you, My will for your life, has yet to be implemented. Expect Me to move. Watch as I accomplish it in you. I will reveal what you need to know when you need to know it. You need truth in the innermost parts of your being. When My truth completely takes over your innermost parts, you will know it. Rejoice in My promise! Lay open your life to Me and let Me move freely in all areas, healing and restoring you. Release your cares and concerns along with your family to Me.

Psalm 34:15, Philippians 2:13, and Psalm 55:22

# Submit Your Will

Portion out your time today to include worship, for I am worthy to be praised. Each day is self-contained and complete in itself. If you could see as I see, then you would know that what you have planned or what you desire cannot fit into your day because your day is already full with My plans for you. Therefore, when you submit your will to Mine and your plans and desires to the ones I have for you, frustration, aggravation, disappointment, anger, and resentment will lose their foothold in you. You will begin to experience the freedom and peace of My rest. Fear and anxiety lose their power in a heart given over to Me. Trust Me to be who I say I am, for there is no turning in Me. From a position of humility, you will seek Me; from a position of love, I will answer.

Proverbs 3:6, Proverbs 19:21, 1 Corinthians 2:9,
and Psalm 56:3

# The Light of Christ

# Be a Harbinger of Spring

Each day brings its own set of joys and sorrows. Rejoice in each day, for I have made them all! Whether you speak to Me or not, I am with you. My rod and My staff are present to lead and guide you. Heaven awaits the moment of fulfillment when My will shall be done on all the Earth. Reach out to those in darkness, and let My light shine through you. Be a harbinger of spring to those whose winter has been long and barren. Spring brings new growth and represents an awakening, signaling hope and promise. Plow the ground, as farmers do in the coolness of the year, and plant your seed.

Psalm 23:4; Isaiah 58:8, 10; and Song of Solomon 2:10–12

# All Things Are Possible

$\mathcal{I}$ am with you, My child. You are right to put your faith in Me. Through Me, all things are possible. Hold on tightly as we move through this time of trouble. It is a deep pit, but My strength never wanes. Believe Me, the darkness enfolds, but My light makes a way. I never change, and My light never dims. You can go forth with confidence: My light will shine in the darkness, and My people will have rest in Me. Wisdom and knowledge come from Me; ask for them, and they are yours. Do not be disturbed by current events. Turmoil will unfold in many households as the enemy gains ground. It has been prophesied from of old. Do not fear, though. I am near and ready to defend My own.

Luke 1:37, 1 John 1:5, James 1:5, and Psalm 50:15

# Share Me with All You Meet

Those who seek Me will find Me. I will not be found in darkness or shadows, for I am the Light. They must come to the Light. When you are in Me, My light surrounds you. Walk in it and bask in the glow. Reflect it onto others: do not keep Me to yourself, but share Me with all you meet. My people wander around lost, without direction, and ignorant of who I am. Show them. Be Me to them. Claim them for Me!

John 12:35 and Romans 12:10

# Put Me First

Hear My voice and pay attention to My words. Prepare your heart for the coming days: fear will grip many, but your confidence is in Me. The coming days will be a burden to many, but your burden will be light. It is My light that shines through you and lights the way for My people. Shine your light for the world to see; it is a beacon of hope in the darkness. Stay open to Me and live out your life for Me so that others will find their way to Me. My glory will be revealed when you put Me first and lay down your life and all you hold dear.

Proverbs 14:26, Matthew 5:16, and 1 Corinthians 10:31

# Walk in the Light of Christ

Look not to the world for the things you need, but look to Me for what you really need. There are no oceans deep enough or mountains high enough to display My glory. But My children walking in the Light of Christ display it for all to see. Walk in the Light and your way will be clear. Bring glory to My name.

Psalm 34:10 and John 8:12

# Time

# All Time Is in My Hands

Heaven rejoices at the sound of My name! I am Lord of All; all creation bows before Me. All time is in My hands. Grass grows, flowers bloom, and lives change all according to My plan, in My time. Do not fret or worry, for I have fashioned time to fit My plan. Your time is still in My hands. Release it to Me. Your struggle with it must cease—you exhaust yourself with something over which you have no control. Use time wisely, and its power over you will cease. Do not mourn its passing but rejoice in its existence! Fill it up with Me, and your days will be full indeed.

Revelation 19:1, Acts 1:7, and 1 Peter 1:24–25

# Spend Time with Me

Walk with Me, My child. Your worth is immeasurable to Me. But you seem to be measuring your value yourself. Look closely at your standards and compare them with Mine. You have met Mine. What you see as lack, I use. Forsake all others for Me. Don't be drawn off course by all that is around you or all that is available to you. Portion out your time: don't look at it as a whole, but break it down. Pick out a site where you will worship Me, and I will meet you there. My heart's desire is to hear your voice lifted up to Me, for you to seek to know Me for who I am. As I reveal Myself to you, your understanding grows and your faith deepens. Turn to Me, not away from Me. What you need is found in Me, not in magazines, television, friends, work, or ministry. Only I can provide what you seek. My heart yearns to connect with yours. Open yourself up to Me, and let Me fill you as nothing else can. My fullness is available at all times and under all circumstances. I am your Adonai. Let Me love you as only I can. I meet all your needs and fill all your spaces. Your time with Me is necessary for the abundant life I provide. It is My joy to fill you up each morning with all you need for the day.

Psalm 68:4, Jeremiah 9:23–24, 1 John 2:16, and Romans 15:13

# My Plan Covers All Circumstances

C all on Me, for I am near and always listening. I have given measures of time to all living things. My people are no different. Each one has a beginning and an end that I have ordained. My plan for each child covers all possible circumstances. I knew your life before you were born; in My love, I have included answers to every question, solutions to every problem, comfort for every hurt, and healing for every wound. Forgiveness is available for every sin. Peace in times of turmoil is yours for the asking, but doubt and disbelief block your path; fear and anxiety prevent you from trusting in Me, the One who saves. Seek Me. Search Me out to discover who I really am. I am revealed in My Word.

Acts 17:26, Psalm 139:15–16, Luke 24:47, and John 1:1, 14

# Measures of Time

he passage of time is meaningless to Me because it is controlled by Me. Do not look at time from your human perspective, but consider it from Mine. I have no deadlines or time constraints because eternity is Mine. Measures of time are necessary for you, though; they give structure and form to your days and give you a starting place for planning and accomplishment. You are restrained by time, but I am not. My plans for you are timeless—not ordered or arranged according to the hours in your day, but according to My perfect will for you. You have a sense that you have "run out of time," but you forget that I am in charge of your time. Trust Me to be your timekeeper. My supply is endless!

Daniel 2:21, Ecclesiastes 3:1, and Acts 17:26–27

# Open Your Gift

Portion out your time according to My direction. Be alert and aware of My leading. Be diligent and have a spirit of excellence as you move through your day. Each day is a gift. If you view them in that way, then you will eagerly anticipate each one. You will experience joy and surprise as each one unfolds, you will find pleasure in what each one holds, and you will feel peaceful and content as each one ends. Do not take your days for granted or waste them, for together they culminate in a life lived. Decide what you will do with the gift of your days. I don't love you less if you waste them or do not accomplish what I have purposed for you, but you do lose or delay the blessing that was prepared for you for that day. Opening a gift requires an effort from the recipient: you have to actively participate to see what's inside and reveal what it holds.

1 Timothy 4:15–16, 1 Timothy 6:6–8,
and Ephesians 5:16–17

# The Promise of Your Days

Each day holds its own promise. Each day is a gift from Me, so treasure it and hold on to it. Make sure to enjoy it as though it is a piece of fruit and drain it of all its juice. Let it go when it's gone and look forward to the next. Do not mourn and grieve the passage of time. It is of no avail. Time is in My hands, and I measure it well. I have allotted time to each person, and I call you to fill your time with Me. You ask Me, "How do I do that?" I want to inhabit each minute, each thought, each decision. You believe that is impossible, but it isn't. When you give Me your day, when you submit your mind, body, will, and emotions to Me, then I take charge of your life in such a way that I inhabit your very being. When you have submitted your thoughts to Me, your words and actions will follow them also. Your will and your emotions will come under My authority, so that each day is filled with Me.

Ecclesiastes 5:18–20 and Psalm 143:8

# Be Purposeful

There is no order to your days. You do only that which is in front of you, without a plan or purpose. But I call you to hold steady on the course I have laid out for you. Do not be distracted by what goes on around you; maintain your balance by seeking My face. Be purposeful with the days that I have given you. Experience the fullness of them. Lay out your tasks so they are visible to you. Complete each one in order and then move on. Take hold of your time and bring it into submission. Do not let time control you, but become the master of the time I have given you. Cast all your cares on Me, the One who saves; I will give you strength to be purposeful.

Psalm 119:1–2, Proverbs 21:5, and Ecclesiastes 11:6

# Manage Your Time

Be aware of the pitfalls and traps that the enemy has laid for you; he does not want you to accomplish your purpose. Manage your time in such a way that there is no waste, using your moments to the fullest. Come to Me to arrange your priorities so that all can be accomplished with ease and grace. With my help, each person who needs your attention will receive what is needed from you, and each task that needs your effort will be accomplished. When you come to Me and follow My Spirit, your thoughts will line up with Mine, and My plans will become yours. I will empower and equip you so that My will is done each day. Follow My instructions so that you accomplish what I have purposed for you to do, My kingdom work. When you are scattered and withdrawn, you lose focus, which causes you to lose your direction. Like a blind person in a forest, you wander around, bumping into trees and getting tangled up in bushes. That is not what I have for you. Walk with confidence and sure steps. Trust Me to be who I say I am. I am all you need.

Psalm 90:12, Galatians 5:16, Ecclesiastes 9:10, and Proverbs 3:26

# Treasure Each Day

Carve out time for Me in your day. Hear My Word and establish it in your heart. Each day I give to you as a gift. Treasure it as such and use it wisely. Fill it up with those things that are joyful, pleasant, productive, and peaceful. Do not mock Me with wasted time. Stay focused on your tasks. Turn to Me for what you need in order to do this. I stand at the ready to help you. I have given you instruction, and I am more than able to provide what you need to carry it out. It is simple and accomplished by obedience.

Psalm 119:38, Proverbs 12:11, and Psalm 18:32

# Trust

# A Flawed Perspective

A seed was planted in you. Let Me tend My garden so that You bear the fruit I have prepared you to bear. My plans for you have not changed. Let Me have My way in you. My desire is to use you for the good of others. Let Me decide what that looks like. When will you completely surrender to Me and My perfect plan? You look at everything through a human perspective, so your interpretation of events and intent is flawed. My perspective is divine and perfect. Please trust Me in this. Continue to walk as I have instructed you: be Me to those I send to you. Rest assured that you will always have enough. I am far from finished, and I know what My next step is—even if you do not. I test your trust in Me. Pass the test. Bow down before Me and release your cares and concerns to Me, the One who saves.

1 Corinthians 3:6–7, Hebrews 6:10, and Isaiah 55:8–9

# I Have Marked Your Territory

You have pleased Me with your prayers. Do not judge your circumstances by what you see, but by faith. Know that I am God and have marked your territory as Mine. Whatever is Mine is covered by My blood, protected by My hand, and provided for by My grace and blessings. Walk according to My Word. You have begun to rightly interpret My Word and apply its truth. Stay in step with Me as we move forward. Seek Me in all things great and small, for all things work together for your good. There is no insignificant activity or insignificant life. All have meaning with Me, and all are meaningful to Me.

Hebrews 11:1, Exodus 12:13, and Matthew 10:30–31

# Heaven Holds the Keys

Heaven alone holds the keys to your life. My hand continues to weave the tapestry of your life. Call on Me for all your needs. I will move in you to align your desires with Mine, which are for your good. Place your hand in Mine so that divine energy flows into you. Give Me your cares, for they wash away in My hands. I am near. Freshen yourself at My well. Lean not on your own understanding, for I will make everything clear as necessary. Do not try to interpret what you see and hear, but wait for My instruction. I am faithful to clarify at the proper time. Seek not your own answers, but trust that Mine are sufficient.

Revelation 1:18, Jeremiah 31:25, and Proverbs 10:17

# Your True Source

Trust in Me, sweet one. Do not be swayed by the movement of the waters around you, for the waters of this time are in constant motion. Waves wash up on shore and then hurry back to their source, only to be thrown back onto the shore. I am your steadfast and true Source. I remain as I have always been: your Strong Tower. I am the Alpha and the Omega. Do not be tossed in the waves, but stay in the calm waters of My embrace. Find your peace in Me.

Ephesians 4:14, Deuteronomy 7:9, Psalm 61:3,
and Revelation 22:13

# Listen for Me

Communication is necessary, for I cannot provide what you need if you do not hear what I say. The ability to hear Me comes when you are willing to listen for Me. Your willingness to listen for Me develops as you focus on Me. When you focus on Me, you will learn who I really am. As you come to know Me, My character will become evident to you: I am loving, gracious, and merciful; I am My Word, and My Word is truth; I am unchanging; omniscient, omnipresent, and omnipotent. This progression produces trust. You must put your trust in Me because it allows Me to move and breathe in you. The first step is to seek Me.

Isaiah 42:23, Ezekiel 37:5–6, and Matthew 6:33

# My Presence Is All You Need

Be still and know that I am God. I go with you every step of the way. Forsake all others for Me. My presence is all you need. Come forth into My light as you step out of your darkness and heed My voice. My soothing tone and hopefilled message will bring you to a place of peace. Trust Me to be who I say I am. What do you lose—pride, arrogance, the illusion of control? What do you gain? You will gain faith, hope, and a love that covers a multitude of sins. You decide which road to take. One leads to life, and the other leads to death.

Psalm 46:10, Matthew 10:37, and Romans 6:16

# I Never Lose Sight of You

Look for Me in all your moments, for you will always find Me. I never hide from My children, although My children try to hide from Me. My all-seeing eyes never lose sight of My Beloved. How could you trust Me if that were not true? Know that I am constantly aware of where you are and what is happening in and around you. I will not interfere, but I will provide what you need to navigate through the landscape of your life.

Isaiah 30:20, Proverbs 15:3, and 2 Peter 1 3

# Rest in Me

Listen to Me, child. Remain in Me, and I will remain in you. Do not doubt My presence or My power in your life. I work continually to fill your mind with My thoughts and desires for your well-being. Satan works continually to fill your mind with doubt and disbelief. Choose in whom you will believe. My way is clear, and you know it. His way is filled with obstacles and confusion. Rest in Me; trust Me. Let Me guide you by My Spirit today, for the Spirit of the Lord will lead you in the way everlasting. Bow before Me and to My will for you. Do what you know is right, and see My power manifest in you. Give glory to your God! Remember, there is no condemnation for those in Christ Jesus.

2 Corinthians 10:5, 1 Corinthians 14:33, and Romans 8:1

# Step Out of Your Comfort Zone

Sacrifice for Me by stepping out of your comfort zone. Let Me feed you and fill you. Don't be afraid. There is so much more I want to show you. You are My precious one, and I love you. I am doing a new thing in you—can't you feel it? Come, take My hand, and walk with Me into your future. I will show you the land of the living. You were once dead in your transgressions, but My love saved you. There is no fear with Me. I will guide you; you won't fall or be destroyed. You will triumph and have freedom in victory. Trust the One who loves you deeply.

Luke 9:23–24, Ephesians 2:4–5, and Psalm 37:24

Truth

# Recognize Truth

S tay on track and keep walking forward. Be obedient to My voice. Never fear, for I am always near. Many will speak, but few will be heard. Learn to discern truth for it is imperative that you know it. If you know the truth, you will know Me. Hold on to Me. Cling to Me. Look neither to the right nor to the left, but put all your hope in Me, for I am faithful and true. My right hand will protect and guide you, and I will fight this battle for you. Do not be dismayed by what is before you, for I am clearing a path, removing all obstructions, so that your way is clear and free from pitfalls.

Luke 11:28, 1 Samuel 17:47, and Isaiah 26:7

# Identify Your Obstacles

What keeps you from Me? What prevents you from seeking My face and desiring My will? How do your circumstances blind you from seeing My hand in your life? Contemplate these questions, because I am ready to reveal truth to you. Identify the rocks in your path and take authority over the ones that obstruct your way; break them up so they cannot hinder your progress. Do not bow down to the rocks in your life, for the rocks cannot hear you. Unlike Me, they are incapable of responding. Recognize the ones that cry out My name, for their purpose is to glorify Me. Without My truth, there are no answers. The world will have answers for you, but remember, I have overcome the world. Therefore, the answers of the world are incomplete, and you will be left without the full knowledge of God.

John 18:37, Hebrews 12:1, Luke 19:40, and John 16:33

# Eternal Truth

Make a way for Me in the hearts and minds of My people. Tokens of affection are not sufficient for Me. Take hold of My truth, for it lives on eternally. The truths of this world change with time and knowledge. What was true in the past may not be true now. But My truth is eternal—never changing. If you seek Me, you will gain My truth and eternity. If you seek the world, you will gain nothing except the present moment. The enemy's lie is that the present moment is the most important. He deceives many in that way. Do not be deceived, My child, but stand and take hold of eternity! Eternity is real, and it is found in Me. Take hold of Me, and you are guaranteed eternity. Blessings on you who know the truth, for you are truly free.

Psalm 111:7–8, Matthew 16:26, and Deuteronomy 33:27

# Delayed Possibilities

Forsake all for me. There are many things that keep you from our time together. Your meandering ways do not eliminate the possibilities; they only delay them. Lay hold of these truths so that you can receive what I have for you and walk in freedom. Joyfully anticipate what is coming. Stand on My Word; it will break the yoke that binds My people. If you could see what is awaiting you, there would be no delay. But I am content to let you delay as you choose.

Luke 14:33, Joshua 1:8, and Isaiah 10:27

# Let Truth Guide You

There is much to be learned through your circumstances. It is important to evaluate the truth separate from your fear. Hold on to the truths you know, and let them guide you as you move forward. Do not be afraid to seek or face the truth. The more that is revealed to you about yourself, the more understanding you will have. Hold fast to My truth. It is your lifeblood, the nourishment for your soul. You are fed by My words that speak to your heart. Your heart is what I seek: open it up to Me so I can make it Mine.

John 17:17, Isaiah 48:17, and Proverbs 23:26

# Stand Firm

The world has many truths that seemingly change with the wind. The shifting winds produce doubt and confusion. My people stand still, wondering which direction to take. I cast My shadow over you as a covering. Make known among people that I am their protection. Hold fast to the truth of My Word. Settle on what is your truth, and stand firm in it.

Colossians 2:8, Isaiah 51:16, and Ephesians 6:14

# Speak Truth at All Times

Pleasant words have no meaning if the heart is not attached to them. Without sincerity, social niceties fall by the wayside. Speak truth at all times, in love. Guarding your tongue does not mean closing your mouth; it means your words need to be vetted for their truth and source before being spoken. If I am your source, then My truth is embedded in your speech. Speak wisdom to My people, for they are ignorant about My truth. Too many voices speak; their ears have become numb and cannot discern the voice of their God. My voice gets drowned out by the many portals used by the enemy to distract and deceive. The enemy uses television, music, the Internet, books, and many classrooms to overwhelm My people with noise and false teachings. Listen to Me, My child. There is only one God, and I am He. Turn and be saved! Allow Me to be Lord of your life. It is only then that you will be able to discern My still, small voice in your heart.

Proverbs 26:24, Proverbs 12:18–19, and Matthew 13:15

# The Truth Is Not in Them

Far higher than any thought or word can imagine, I sit on My throne in Heaven. Visit Me in My temple. Leave your burdens and kneel before Me. They will be gone when you are finished. Mere words cannot convey who I am and how I love you. Weary are the people who cannot hear, for they are unable to speak what they do not know. Their eyes have been blinded, their ears have been closed, and their hearts have been darkened by sin. The truth is not in them, so it cannot be spoken by them. Their answer is the very thing they reject, but My love remains and is for all.

Matthew 8:2, Matthew 13:13, and 1 John 4:9–10

# A Covering

Study My Word so you can speak it to My people. Seek Me for instruction and meaning. Let Me teach you My way. My truth is different from the world's. The world's truth comes from knowledge, but My truth is born out of My Spirit and is divine. I reign over all; therefore, what goes out from My Spirit is a covering for My people. My truth is a covering, and under that covering, you are free from all evil. The enemy holds sway over this world, but not over My people. Under the covering of My truth, you gain ground. It is gained first within yourself, then through you as you touch others for Me.

Proverbs 4:13 and Zechariah 8:16

# Your Foundation

Hold fast to the truths you have been taught. They will stand you in good stead as you make your way through the day. Capture your thoughts and bring them into submission to Me, for they tend to lead you down paths of unrighteousness. Take hold of My truths so that your path is straight. Plank upon plank have been laid out to strengthen your path. Walk firmly and confidently on the foundation of My truth. Study My Word that you may know My truth.

Psalm 15:2–3 and 1 John 2:24

# Wisdom

# Divine Wisdom

Wisdom and knowledge are not the same. A person can have much worldly knowledge but no wisdom. Another can have My wisdom but very little knowledge. Divine wisdom always overcomes lack of knowledge. My wisdom can be yours, but it is only found in Me. If it is in Me, you have to seek Me, find Me, and enter into My presence to obtain it. This is not difficult, but it takes effort and perseverance. Make decisions that will draw you closer to Me. Call on Me in your doubt or confusion. Clarity comes as you seek My face. Wisdom comes as you prepare the way. My peace follows in the perfect order of these. Persevere, My sweet one! I am not a mountain to be climbed but a door to be opened. Enter in! I await you.

1 Corinthians 1:20 and John 10:9

# Financial Wisdom

Hold on to what you have. Don't throw it away on meaningless things. Think and pray before you spend anything. Bring it before Me, and let Me advise you. Do not relax, but stay alert. The enemy will snatch away your stores if you are not aware. Be careful and watchful, for his ways are cunning. I will always provide. You must be diligent and excellent in your ways. Give when I say give and keep when I say keep. Spend within reason and for your enjoyment. Do not indulge your flesh with unproductive purchases. You will know what those are as you continue to seek My wisdom in these matters.

Luke 12:15, 1 Timothy 6:18, and Matthew 13:22

# My Wisdom Is Life Changing

We meet in the middle of your praise and your prayers. You speak your heart to Me, and I speak Mine to you. Do not forget who I am. We are joined eternally. My plans are not just for this moment but for all of your moments. Pass on the secrets you have been given. They are more precious than gold or silver. They are more beautiful and valuable than rubies and diamonds. My wisdom is life changing, mind-altering, and brings joy and hope to those who hear it. You are not perfect, My child, but you are perfectly placed in time and position to accomplish what I have ordained for you. As with the prophet Jeremiah, I am with you, and My presence will protect you. Be mindful of your weaknesses so that you are never caught off guard. The devil waits for openings and watches for opportunities. Give him none.

Psalm 146:2, Daniel 2:30, and Jeremiah 1:19

# Grow in Wisdom

You are My child, in whom I am well pleased. Let us walk together as in the comfort of old friends. Be mindful of My desire to spend time with you and talk with you. Open your ears to hear Me, for I will speak at all times. I give words of knowledge when I speak. Receive them into your spirit. Grow with the wisdom I give you. Let it take over and rule your heart and mind. There is victory on the horizon! Move toward the light, for the dawn of that day is near. Be not discouraged by the discord that surrounds you. Keep moving forward. You are learning more and more about yourself as I reveal yourself to you. Use your understanding to seal the changes you've made. Harbor no ill will as you move along the path to freedom and victory. Do what I have asked of you in regard to making amends with others. Your path is straight, so walk in it.

John 15:15; Proverbs 2:1, 5; and 2 Peter 1:8

# Your First Love

Welcome home, My child. You have come back to your first love. I am pleased to have your ear again. I don't hold it against you, because that is not My nature. So let us move on from here. Press into Me for your wisdom and direction. You have the keys; use them. Heaven rejoices at what is about to happen! A new thing is taking place that the world has never seen. Remain in Me and be a part of My work. There is plenty to do, and the laborers are few. Present yourself to Me as a clean vessel: one empty of self and ready to be filled with the One who desires to live within you. Let Me fill you with what I have for you. It will far outshine anything you can imagine.

Revelation 2:4, Matthew 9:37, and 2 Corinthians 9:8

# Do Not Grow Weary

ou who are weary will be rewarded if you do not give up.
The prize is in reach. Hang on and do not let go of what
you have. The struggle continues, but your offering will
be met with praise and honor. Do not grow weary of doing good,
for Heaven awaits at the end. The end will bring peace and joy
to all who complete the journey. We are waiting. Do not waste
what I have given you. Places and people fade away, but My gifts
remain. Use them wisely. Wisdom comes from time invested with
Me. Your investment produces more than what you put in. I will
always give more to you than you give to Me. That is how it should
be, considering who We are. I bless you in many ways over and
above what you deserve. How else could I humble you?

2 Chronicles 15:7, Proverbs 2:6, and Psalm 57:10

# Worth and Value

# Be Pure and Holy

resent yourself holy and pure, as I am holy and pure. I am not calling you to be perfect but to walk in purity and holiness. You do this through Me. I fill you with My Spirit, and He makes you holy and pure. Do not be alarmed at My words; they are true. You do not see yourself as I see you, so it is difficult to imagine yourself as pure and holy. But you are My workmanship; I have crafted you in My image. I see what you cannot. Your very heart, which I have made, is seen and known by Me.

2 Corinthians 7:1, Genesis 1:27, and 1 Kings 8:39

# Beauty Is in the Eye of the Beholder

Your skin is only an outer covering for your heart. Keep your heart in shape; you must nurture it because it stores who you really are. Your skin will wear out, as it is meant to. It is an outward picture of time passing. Your time is in My hands. Do not look in the mirror for evidence of your beauty; it is fading as it ought. Beauty is in the eye of the beholder. Look into My eyes for what you seek. You are precious in My sight, and your beauty is within your heart and spirit. As you age, people will no longer look at the outward evidence of it; they will be drawn to what I have placed in you. Be content with who you are in Me.

Proverbs 4:23, I Samuel 16:7, and I Peter 3:3—4

# You Are a New Creation

You are a new creation in Christ Jesus! Look into My eyes and see your true reflection. I will show you what you really look like on the inside. You have believed the enemy's lies that you are unacceptable, and therefore, you do not take care of yourself. You are completely acceptable to Me. Your body is My temple, so you must take care of it. All that I have given you—everything you own and all that you are—is precious in My sight. Honor Me by taking care of yourself and your possessions.

2 Corinthians 5:17, I Corinthians 6:19–20, and Isaiah 43:4

# Your Worth and Value

Measure your worth and value by My standards, not human standards. You were worth giving My life for. How valuable does that make you? I want you to rest in the knowledge that I hold you in high esteem even when others do not. Believe Me when I say to you that you are My beloved—well loved, cared for, and protected by Me.

John 3:16 and Daniel 10:19

# Your Path

# Step onto Your Path

Make a way for Me in the desert, as I have made a way for you. The land is parched and dry and in need of refreshment. Be My vessel that I use to pour Myself out on the people who walk on the dry and barren ground. There are many paths laid out, but only one is for you. I have prepared the way for you to go, and it has been lit for you. You see it, so walk in it. Step out and onto your path.

Isaiah 40:3 and Proverbs 4:18

# Choose Life

The path you have walked without Me was laid out by another. That path leads away from Me, and I have no part in it. Therefore, you must choose. Choose wisely with whom you will walk. The enemy's way seems good and proper, but it leads to death. Spiritual death precedes physical death. He has to destroy your spirit before he can destroy you. So be on your guard around those things that appear good. Examine them closely for authenticity. Question the value of your choices. I will never take away your right to choose, but I urge you to examine your motives and contemplate the outcome.

Ephesians 2:1–2, Proverbs 14:12, and Deuteronomy 30:19

# The Journey

Mirrors are used to reflect an image. What do you see when you look into the mirror of My eyes? You see who I made you to be. You see yourself as I see you: beautiful, pure, whole, and complete. It is who you are becoming. Rejoice in that truth! Do not give up or grow weary of the journey. Your destination is perfect. Your journey includes pruning and refining. It also includes peace and joy. There are obstacles and challenges, but there are also victories and successes. You will make wrong choices and experience failure, but you will also make wise decisions and triumph over adversity. Life was not meant to be uneventful. It was meant to be lived to the full with Me. Taste and see the goodness of the Lord!

Hebrews 10:14, Isaiah 40:31, and Psalm 16:11

# Let Go of the Past

My heart is for you. Listen to My voice as I whisper instructions to you. Your way has been laid out from the beginning of time. Walk it out. Try to measure how far you have come. You cannot measure it, but you know it is real. My work in you has occurred over time to align with My plan for you. All things work together for your good. Each day of your life and each step of your journey were known to Me before you were born. I have ordained the moments of your life to be overlaid by and connected to the lives of others for My purposes. Therefore, you have experienced joy and pain and loss and gain as these people have entered and left your life. It is not wise to hold on to people and things whose purpose has been fulfilled. When this happens, you do not have the ability to embrace who or what I have prepared for you next. Opportunities for pruning, growth, and joy are missed because you are turned in the wrong direction. When you look backward and hold on to what was, you miss what is and what can be. Let go of your past with the people and events that populate it. Turn and face your future with hope and joy. When you do this, you become present in each of your moments, and then no opportunity is missed or lost.

Ecclesiastes 3:1, Romans 8:28, Isaiah 43:18,
and Proverbs 23:18

# I Am Patient

atience is necessary as I do My work in you. My actions are coupled with your responses. How and when you respond determines My next action. If you are quick to be obedient, we move forward at a faster pace. If you hold back, we stay in this place longer. You always get to choose the pace. I determine the path. No effort goes unnoticed or unrewarded. You are not hidden from Me.

Joshua 5:6, Proverbs 16:9, and 1 Corinthians 15:58

# Wisdom

*L*et it be known that I am the Lord of all. Pass on My wisdom to all who come. Divine wisdom is food for those who are hungry; it is water for those who thirst. Eat your fill and quench your thirst at My table. Listen, My child! Do not reject the cornerstone, for the building will crumble without the right foundation. Hear Me and do not turn away, for eternity awaits your answer. How will you answer My call? Will you answer? Do not deny Me the pleasure of your company. I am in relentless pursuit of My Beloved. Take My hand and walk with Me. Our path together is known only by Me, because I laid it out before you were born.

John 6:35, Matthew 21:42, and Luke 19:10

# About The Author

Lydia B. Talley earned an MA from Louisiana State University and became a school counselor in 1995. She is now a licensed Christian counselor with a private practice in Baton Rouge, Louisiana. She specializes in serving the spiritual and emotional needs of patients suffering from trauma.

Lydia has been married to John Talley Jr. for twenty-five years, and they have four children between them: Laurie, Michael, Julie, and Trey. Lydia and John are blessed with seven grandchildren and one great-grandchild.